SHAKESPEARE'S SONNETS

the
ALTERNATIVE TEXT

Derived from re-paging
according to the Notebook Sonnets

S.C. Campbell

The text of the Sonnets here printed is the same as that of
Shakespeare's Sonnets Edited as a Continuous Sequence
(Bell & Hyman 1978). The case for the validity of this text has been
radically re-examined and is submitted to the judgement of the
general as well as the academic reader.

SHAKESPEARE'S SONNETS

the
ALTERNATIVE TEXT

published by
Cassandra Press 2009

ISBN 0 9554 193 1 X
ISBN 978 0 9554.193 1 7

being the third edition of
Shakespeare's Sonnets Edited as a Continuous Sequence,
first edition Bell & Hyman (UK) 1978

ISBN 0 7135 1857 X (cased)
ISBN 0 7135 1858 8 (limp)

Rowman & Littlefield (USA) 1979

ISBN 0 8476 6134 2

Second edition Cassandra Press 1999

ISBN 0 950 8829 5 X

Typeset by N. Beeson, NAB Services
Printed by Piggott Black Bear (Cambridge) Ltd

Correspondence for the Cassandra Press should be addressed to
N Beeson, Piggott Black Bear (Cambridge) Ltd,
347 Cherry Hinton Road, Cambridge CB1 8DH

ACKNOWLEDGEMENTS

Since the first edition of this text with different commentary was published in 1978, much of my gratitude is owed to people who are no longer alive. To two Classics Professors, Madge Dale, my Oxford tutor, and her husband Tom Webster, who prevailed on New Hall Cambridge to take me in when the Fleet Street paper, *The New Chronicle*, for which I worked, went brankrupt, paying the price of its liberalism to cold war fear of anything that split the anti-socialist vote. To Graham Storey, Trinity Hall Director of Studies in English, who let me share the teaching of his students for two decades; to Helena Shire of Robinson College who helped and encouraged, as did Margaret Braithwaite and Professor Dorothy Emmet who published me in their periodical *Theoria to Theory*; to astronomer Hubert Linfoot and philosopher Renford Bambrough who countenanced my thinking about probability (as against those who mock any rearrangement of the Sonnets); to Peter Pears, who called this text of the Sonnets "the best I know" when reading from it in Orford Church on 17th June 1985. (*Gay News* had disliked my edition). I worked with Peter during the last two months of his life at his project to record this whole text for Hyperion.

I owe less backward-looking gratitude to Lucy Cavendish College who gave me a Research Fellowship while I was preparing my two-volume 1978 edition; to Queens College student Peter Roberts who came to me with a First in Classics and left with a First in English, and was so interested in my thinking about the Sonnets that I decided to make it a serious project; to George Steiner who trusted his Greek Tragedu students to me when he went abroad; to Simon Kingston who as Literary Editor for George Bell & Sons accepted this text, saw it through its first edition and has been tireless in trying to get it a better hearing; to Professor John Bayley and to fine Shakespeare scholar Barbara Everett of Somerville College for backing my work before and after publication; to Jeffrey Wood for devoted advocacy when he was teaching for Cambridge Long Road Sixth Form College; to staunch friend, counsellor and poet, Sally Graves (Chilver), and Brian Fall, her successor as LMH Principal; poet Anne Stevenson and tenor Ian Partridge for faith in my poetic judgement; to Stephen Barber for his beautiful solution to the problem of Q96; to Professor Alastair Fowler for wise advise and his rare ability to see value in views different from his own; to Roberta Staples, Librarian of Lady Margaret Hall for the warmth and width of her sympathy with creative and scholarly ventures; to my generous friend of four decades, Michael Cartwright who founded Piggott Printers, and to Nikki Beeson of Piggott Black Bear (Cambridge) Ltd for her indefatigable computer skills and patient good nature.

S.C. Campbell
Cambridge, England

CONTENTS

W.S. the Droeshout engraving   *H.W. The Hilliard miniature*

INTRODUCTION

I *Summary of what happened*

Shakespeare's sonnets tell a true story which has both drama and tragedy.

He tells us to whom they are addressed. It would have been an impossible social gaffe to describe as "Adonis" in sonnet Q53 anyone other than the young earl of Southampton, Henry Wriothesley, for and about whom his best-selling long poem *Venus and Adonis* had been written. It was published in 1593, when the poet was 29, married and a father, and his patron was 20, a Hamlet-like personality in other ways besides evoking the author's affection: stage-struck, hostile to women and marriage and pining for a father-figure since he had lost his own in childhood, after being taken from his mother and taught to hate her. After his father's death he lived with her again; he closely resembled her, as portraits show and sonnet Q3 remarks.

Titchfield Abbey near Southampton was the earl's main home, and an obvious place of refuge for him and his entourage while plague gripped London and closed the theatres between 1592 and 1594. The great house, whose fine stonework can still be admired, had a first floor 'Playhouse Room' where legend says Romeo and Juliet (an early play) was acted, and had ample grounds for the park-land setting of *Love's Labours Lost*, a send-up of fellow protégés whom Shakespeare will have had the chance to get to know while his patron "one early morn did shine with all-triumphant splendour on my brow" (Q33). That would also have provided the chance to learn what Bottom and Sly know of luxurious living, to meet top people on such terms that he could always portray them in his plays as real people, and not least to gain first-hand acquaintance with the Renaissance ferment of ideas and values. Touring actors must in any case have seen as little of their wives as sailors do, so he may well have become the earl's poet-in-residence as an alternative livelihood during the plague. The distinguished scholar Florio had similar status in Southampton's household.

The second best-selling long poem written at this time, *The Rape of Lucrece,* opened with the words "the love I dedicate to your lordship is without end": a striking contrast to the opening of *Venus and Adonis* "I know not how I shall offend . . ." *The Lucrece* preface hints that a third dedication has been commissioned; the Notebook Sonnets Q77 and Q122 suggest that this was the

Sonnets. These recurrently assert that there has been a lifelong commitment by both men. Qs 9-10 find a graceful way of telling that the younger man fell in love first - and in view of the difference in rank only he could have altered the footing on which they stood. Q10 line 1 along with line 13 "for love of me" implies that Q9.13's charge 'you love no-one' has been rebutted with 'you know I love you'. The counter-pledge by the poet "for love of you" comes marginally later, in Q15.13. That the opening sonnets urge marriage on the young man reflects that hereditary rank made that a social duty.

Lucrece was published in the spring of 1594. Within months there was a "vulgar scandal" (Q112), in the shape of two publications which warned the friends against homosexuality with clear identification of both men, namely Chapman's *The Shadow of Night* in its Part II and the anonymous *Willobie His Avisa*. The latter was a cryptic succès de scandale which ran through many editions, and appeared towards its close to claim royal authority for its complaint that England was becoming a den of unnatural vice (its actual wording is ruder than that). This topic could have seemed of national importance because King James of Scotland would soon succeed the ageing Elizabeth, and he was known to be gay, for example by his Phoenix poem (published in 1591).

The highborn friend's reputation must be safeguarded at the cost of the poet's own, Q36 grants in touching acceptance of being publicly cold-shouldered; both men had shed private tears together over this (Q34). The mood changes from poem to poem. The stolen mistress is a legal fiction to give decorum to the theme of unfaithfulness. *Avisa's* main target was H.W. (Southampton's initials); W.S. was side-lined, although the first page mentions *Lucrece*. But Chapman's poem flattered the aristocrat - "wealth fawns on fools, virtues are meat for vices" - and made Shakespeare, identified by the Ovid quotation he prefaced to *V. and A.*, essentially the sole scapegoat. So any subsequent patronage of Chapman by H.W. would have amounted to endorsing this gross injustice.

That appears to have happened in Q86.13. Farewell is immediately said in Q87, followed by some of the most passionately bitter poems ever written. The Quarto text blunts by its illogical disorder (see p. xi) the degree of this bitterness. It obscures that the poet's offsetting offence foretold in Q88 was a mistake of identity, between opposites which for sanity's sake (as for Troilus in 5.ii. 135-158) need to be kept as far apart as heaven and hell: between the friend's feminine persona and a whore, between Plato's spiritual love which is 'fair' (cf. the white horse of the *Phaedrus*) and sexuality at its blackest, unaware that there is any difference between one owner of "will" and another (Q136), the loathly lady of myth and witchcraft who is Lust (Q129) personified, offensive to all five senses (Q141), to whom both men are now enslaved. The witchcraft phantom was originally the friend's shadow-self (she fast deteriorates), and the first poem addressed to H.W. Clapham's, *Narcissus*, saw him as in love with his own shadow. So with the poet that adds up to an eternal triangle, which takes a very funny form in the brief light relief of Q143.

Mistaken identity is Shakespeare the dramatist's favourite - and deeply charitable - way of accounting for infidelity. "Believe me, King of Shadows, I mistook!" There are those who would say Puck here offers a tenable account of the homosexual mind-set, that it mistakes a male for a female, who is what it really desires. But the Sonnets say the opposite: it is the female who defrauds, not from his patron's sexist standpoint but because of the profoundly individual character of his affection: the real beloved was a real male. The plays show how far Shakespeare was from being a woman-hater (see pp. xxi - xxii).

A classical scholar once wrote "Either this emendation is correct or I am a great poet". The present editor is nothing like a great enough poet to have invented the core sequence about the poet's offence which is clued by the re-paging, Qs. 113, 114, 148, 147, 129, 130 (pp. 103-8 scc pp. 161, 171).

The re-ordered text recovers from delusion and ends movingly in reconciliation, but there is every reason to doubt that this happened in real life. Indeed that could be one reason why he sabotaged the ending in the eventual publication. There are constant fierce or sad references to betrayed friendship in the plays. He could not say as his notebook text had said "I told my wrath, my wrath did end": message not received.

Before charging Southampton with cowardice or hypocrisy one should realise that defying the throne or the powers behind it was hazardous, and he very nearly paid the uttermost farthing. In 1600 he joined in the rebellion led by his close friend Essex (whose cousin he had very recently married and fathered a child by). The rebellion failed, and he was sentenced to death. He spoke in his own defence in Westminster Hall - "He spake very well, but methought somewhat too much" wrote John Chamberlain, "as a man that would fain live". Could Shakespeare have heard this, or at least a report of it, and been moved to write in his later play *Measure for Measure* Claudio's impassioned outburst against his death sentence?

The sentence on the earl was commuted to imprisonment. After three years in the Tower he was released by King James on his accession and returned to high public favour and status. One of the first things he did was to mount a production of *Love's Labours Lost* at his London home. It was by then a published play (though the first three Acts seem truncated). There is no evidence of any renewed contact over this with Shakespeare. Was it perhaps he who refused it? He was writing at the time the most bitter of all his plays, *Timon of Athens*. "Timon will to the woods, where he shall find The unkindest beast more kinder than mankind." The Sonnets were not published until 1609, arguably in a bowdlerised form dictated mainly by the need to avoid or minimise libel. Readers since then have recurrently felt that the poems are in the wrong order. One cannot know enough to do justice to a life, but a work of art speaks for itself.

II *What is wrong with the Quarto text?*

Sonnets Q100-126		Sonnets Q127-154
A.	Eight symptoms of disease & disaster, recovery described	The same eight symptoms, onset described
B.	Forgiveness asked for a recent offence against the friend, falling for a worse love	An offence by the poet against the friend takes place, falling for a worse love
C.	The Muse is reproached for a lapse into a "dark" and "base" theme and told to return to the friend	The friend is displaced for 28 sonnets by a "dark" and "base" addressee

CONCLUSION

The order of the two columns is wrong and should be reversed.

There is no obligation on a sonnet writer to make connected sense on any scale beyond that of fourteen lines. But when there are sense connections between sonnets there is every obligation on the reader to notice them.

III   *The Notebook and the Two Series, and matters arising*

"Thy gift, thy tables", Sonnet Q122. "Tables", "tablets" and "table-book" meant a notebook of empty pages, such as Hamlet kept in his doublet for jotting down his thoughts (*Ham* I.V. 107). A large example from the sixteenth century can be seen in the Rare Books Room of the Cambridge University Library. This has one sonnet of unspecified authorship written out by hand on each page, i.e. two to a leaf, with no wasted pages. The 1609 text of the Sonnets could have been derived from such a notebook, paged as it is here, if it had some leaves cut out, chiefly the two sections about the stolen mistress, and some of the leaves reversed, and if the compositor finding a batch of cut-out leaves placed between two closely linked sonnets, Q27 and Q28, had the common sense to set them both before setting the loose pages. The sonnet on the verso of Q28 would then get displaced without a page-partner, to follow the last leaf of the cut-out material, without invalidating the two-to-a-leaf assumption.

Such a notebook would not have been cheap - no excuse for wasting any pages. 'Thy gift' means given by the poems' addressee. That one was given as a commission for the sonnets is suggested by the two Notebook Sonnets in conjunction with a hint in the *Lucrece* dedication "What I have done is yours, what I have to do is yours", which implies that a third dedication has been commissioned. Sonnet Q23.9 makes clear that his sonnets are addressed to the same person as "my books", his two long poems (he did not sign published plays until 1598 and never dedicated any). To alter "my books" in Q23 to "my looks", as some who reject Southampton as the addressee have done, is without any textual justification and misses the main point being made, that written work despite being a dumb-show can be more eloquent because more privately and honestly explicit than words spoken in public: the metaphor of a private exchange of glances between lovers is kept for the lovely final couplet.

The first 'notebook sonnet', Q77, comes exactly half way through the Quarto text and refers to "these waste blanks", "the vacant leaves . . . of this book", which is called in the last line "thy book". The contents of the first half of the book is finally deprecated, as an author is entitled to belittle his own work, by inviting the addressee to fill the rest with something better. The poet is wishing or offering to resign his commission half way through. The sonnets this edition calls Series Two resume until the "vacant leaves" are full, an obvious inference from "full-character'd" in the second 'notebook sonnet' Q122. So the book containing the half-done task was given back to the poet by its addressee as so to speak returned work, and Series Two at once records the patron complaining of his poet's silence.

It is obvious that what is implied is one notebook with a fresh start half way through. When this text was first published, a review in a leading scholarly journal alleged that it postulated *two* notebooks. This mis-statement completely undermined the support derived from the Notebook Sonnets for the edition's text and main theses. This new edition aims at readership by the general public in the hope of less prejudicial reception.

The second 'notebook sonnet', Q122, is called "thy record", in the sense of a memoir of him as well as a book that he had given, and it is now "full-character'd with lasting memory" in the poet's brain and heart, where it is more indelible than in the "idle rank" or inferior category of thing which is a bookful of words. The poet knows all its contents by heart, so he has given it away and is not re-presenting it to its addressee, presumably judging its contents unsuitable. He could have sent a copy of this sonnet separately. Assuming it was the last of the even-numbered total of 154 sonnets it would have had a blank verso in the notebook and can therefore be relocated from its Quarto position without a page-mate. For, taking the first recto in the notebook as having been a dedication and placing Q1 on the first verso, one gets nearly all the closely paired twins of sonnets onto facing pages, whose invitation to write in pairs must surely have been what encouraged the poet to do so. The notebook could have been given to the private friends that Meres mentioned in a book published in 1598 - "his sugar'd sonnets among his private friends". Sugar'd does not mean sugary but suggests a gilded pill, and may reflect the powerful element of reproach in the poems. Cf. 2 *Hen.* VI 3 ii 45 "Hide not thy poison with such sugared words."

Series I accepted public cold-shouldering by the patron-friend with a moving patience (Q36); the friend had wept over it, Q34. Why then does Series II say a stark "Farewell" (Q 87.1) immediately after the rival poets theme which seems a lesser ground of complaint?

The sonnet that immediately precedes "Farewell", Q86, is about a team of rivals, a living poet being helped night by night by a greater ghost. So much greater that one may guess the first two lines were written about Marlowe before his death and the sonnet was later rewritten. For this dual authorship transparently suggests *Hero and Leander*, the completion of which Chapman embarked on after Marlowe's violent accidental death in 1593. Chapman alleged in his Sestiad III, 183 ff. that Marlowe's ghost helped him write it. His part of the poem was not published until 1598, but he could well have made the boast verbally to reinforce his claim to write the continuation. He also claimed in Sestiad III 191 that Marlowe promised him half of the enterprise, which is absurd since not forseeing his violent death the greater poet would have meant to finish it himself. If Southampton did anything to "countenance" (Q86.13) Chapman, for example by authorising him to take up the probably friendly rivalry of Marlowe's Leander with Shakespeare's Adonis for the "prize" of the most popular patron of the time, it would have been an insufferable insult to Shakespeare. And not only because it robbed English literature of the glorious chance of a Marlowe-Shakespeare work.

For Chapman was the author of one of the two 1594 publications called Hymns, *The Shadow of Night*, which (in its second part) made scandalous aspersions on the cross-class patron-and-poet relationship. It says nothing worse about one of them than that "noblesse stoops sometimes beneath his blood", with warnings against homosexuality couched in mythical terms which apart from Ganymede are fairly obscure. But Chapman uses transparent plurals to abuse "flesh-confounded souls" while obviously identifying Shakespeare (in *Hymn to Cynthia* 162-5) by way of the Ovid quotation prefaced to *Venus and Adonis*. Since any erotic aspect of the friendship could obviously not have been initiated by the socially subordinate man, for Chapman's poem to make Shakespeare the scapegoat was most unjust, and was made far worse if the earl did anything which appeared to endorse that by approval of Chapman. The scapegoat sonnet Q89 is one of the most powerful of them all in its bitterness, equalled by the superb equivocation between self-accusation and self-vindication in Q49. Southampton was not in the end the recipient of Chapman's 1598 dedication, perhaps because on juster reflection he was not willing to be, but it could have been he as Marlowe's intended dedicatee who gave Chapman permission to write the continuation and so "countenanced" him (Q86.13). Q85.7 mentions a "Hymn" by the rival.

Fortunately for us jealousy inspired Chapman to rare heights of graphic description in his prose dedication to both parts of Hymnus in Noctem. Using transparent plurals he gives the most vivid picture that survives of Shakespeare as a social and literary success, doubtless in the early days when the friend's sun shone "with all triumphant splendour on my brow" (Q33). Chapman "marvels" (in modernised spelling) "to see passion-driven men, reading but to curtail a tedious hour, and altogether hidebound with affection to great men's fancies, take upon them as killing censures as if they were judgement's Butchers, or as if the life of truth lay tottering in their verdicts".

"Hide-bound" echoes Robert Greene's 1592 attack on Shakespeare which misquoted 3 *Hen*. VI iv 137 "O tiger's heart wrapt in a woman's hide" by ending the line "a player's hide", and continued "who thinks himself the only Shake-scene in a country!" For "judgement's Butchers" compare Nashe's soubriquet for Shakespeare 'Kilcow' (surprisingly perhaps, the portrait of Nashe as Moth in *L.L.L.* seems affectionate). The story was widely told that when he had to kill a calf for his farmer father he made a speech over it first, while it tottered awaiting its death. Probably the speech will have been an apology for killing, in view of his strong sympathy for animals. See the touching description of killing a calf in 2 *Hen*. VI. 3. i. 21.

Chapman's next paragraph, again using transparent plurals, has the would-be literary pundit either damning something with faint praise or excusing himself for liking something perhaps not first class - he "squeamishly commends it for a pretty toy". He is then accused of mercenary as well as passionate motives. (The Sonnets don't conceal that livelihood as well as the life of the heart is at stake.) Of course the man could show off before an audience, he was an actor. He was also marvellously good company - "Hadst thou not played some kingly parts in sport. Thou hadst been a companion for a king" (John Davies about Shakespeare, Epigram 159). Flatterers are not good company. Ben Jonson praised him for his "open and free nature". Among the rhetorical hyperboles of the sonnets - he needed to show that he could write the way the culture snobs thought proper - and the instances of ironic double-speak, there are sudden moments of heart-stopping sincerity. It is ironic to call himself a "slave" during the "sad interim" he has mentioned in Q56, just because he must watch the clock for his employer and not ask personal questions; the real effect of this is to show how far from slavery the relationship used to be.

> "Nor dare I question with my jealous thought
> Where you may be, or your affairs suppose,
> But like a sad slave stay and think of nought
> Save where you are, how happy you make those."   (Q57)

The other much more widely read scandal published in 1594 shortly after *Lucrece*, *Willobie His Avisa*, mentions Shakespeare's *Lucrece* on its first page but its chief target was 'H.W.' Every friendship is an interaction of two characters. Henry Wriothesley 3rd Earl of Southampton, to whom *Lucrece* was dedicated, has been briefly characterised on p.vii Hostile to marriage, he angered the powerful Lord Burleigh at the beginning of the 1590's by refusing to marry his granddaughter. The earliest poem written about him called him Narcissus. Recurrent hints from contemporary sources that he was homosexual are doubtless the reason why other candidates for the Sonnets' addressee have been canvassed in defiance of Q.53 line 5, along with English class-consciousness which cannot believe that a cross-class friendship could be sincere. Shakespeare was in fact remarkably egalitarian, partly no doubt thanks to the initial genuineness of this friendship ("Take it for your own fault and not mine" says a common soldier - William S! to King Henry V who was also Falstaff's "Hal").

Southampton was well educated - St John's Cambridge and Gray's Inn - cultured, a patron of all the arts - music saddened him, as it did Jessica in the wonderful passage about the music of the spheres (*M. of V.* 5. i. 69ff). He had a large library, and as resident tutor and scholar the polymath Florio. Southampton's signature would take five minutes to write, see the letter about the need of repairs to Beaulieu Abbey which Hugh Calvert photocopied in his *Shakespeare's Sonnets* p. 226. It has been mooted that Shakespeare acted as secretary in this letter (see Q10.7's reference to the beauteous roof that was in danger of ruin). Shakespeare had trained as a lawyer's scrivener, perhaps forseeing that he would need to write out some millions of his own words - could the dizzy signature on the will be due to writer's cramp? Jeunesse dorée tends to be lazy; if the poet-secretary was recruited to take notes on sessions with Florio that would help to explain how Shakespeare acquired so much knowledge and understanding of classicial literature and thought.

Avisa's slander if "vulgar" (Q112) was decidedly cryptic. The heroine is by a double Latin pun a "bird" which is "never seen", never instanced, because her claim to be so chaste that she never even sleeps with her own husband is disbelieved. She may on other levels of the meaning be a whore. She is not except grammatically a woman, she is a phoenix; one of the illustrations shows a bird's claw protruding beneath her skirt. The legendary phoenix had to be celibate because it was the only creature of its kind alive at any one time. It had acquired a turtle as partner by Elizabethan times, and in post-classical Greece it stood for homosexual practises far from the ideal of sublimation and celibacy which the Phoenix Queen revived and endorsed when she married her country with a ring.

In the Elizabethan as in other ages this ideal was doubtless more honoured in the breach than in the observance. But a genuinely religious culture can affirm ideals which it falls short of, without hypocrisy. Shakespeare hated hypocrisy in proportion to his love of faithfulness, yet he does not repudiate Plato's ideal that 'heavenly love' should be able to dispense with a carnal yoke-mate, that "marriage of the mind" is worth more than the aspects of marriage which are subject to "impediments", ecclesiastical or other. The end of *Venus and Adonis* makes sodomy a lethal act. The boar "thought to kiss him, and hath killed him so" by sheathing its tusk in his body (lines 1110ff). Shakespeare certainly knew Montaigne's essay which idealised male friendships; one third of his poem *The Phoenix and the Turtle* is a close paraphrase of Florio's translation of that essay into English. Accepted now into a culturally elite circle he would certainly have known landmarks of Greek thought transmitted to the educated by the Renaissance, such as Plato's distinction in the *Phaedrus* between the white horse of spiritual love and the black horse of carnal love. So he cannot have failed to have this in mind in sonnet Q51; yet it puns on "neigh" and "nay" in line 11 and its brilliantly equivocal ending either pensions off the inferior horse or gives it the go-ahead. This could have been written to amuse a gay friend; but Q121 is not equivocal, if rather difficult to construe ("so deemed" in line 3 must mean "deemed vile"); it declares a different code in matters of "will" (which then could mean sex) from those who criticise him, but "By their rank thoughts my deeds must not be shown", unless they maintain that right conduct in this sphere is simply not possible for fallen man. Q42.3 may be a sincere preference by the older man; support in his life's work and destiny may have mattered more than the erotic aspect of their friendship. The younger man's preference may have been the other way, hence his readiness for a total breach if the love affair was proscribed by authority. Modern reductive thought may side against the poet over this, and rhyme Socrates with prick-tease for persuading all those young men that talking philosophy was the finest way of making love. While 'Pandemos' (vulgar) Aphrodite need never progress beyond "cried O and mounted" (*Cymbelne* II v 17), Platonism seems to have been least tolerant of the goddess when she patronised only gender difference, arguably because individual difference can then be ignored or dismissed as inferiority. Sex is generic, 'Ouranios' or heavenly love is individual. So Montaign, "If I am asked why I loved him, I can only say, because it was he, because it was myself". *Avisa* alleged and deplored a growing late Elizabethan trend towards homosexuality; Marlowe's reputed saying "All they that love not tobacco and boys are fools" confirms the trend while sounding as much sardonic as commendatory. Yet it cannot be denied that this was the greatest epoch in the history of English poetry. (No-one should infer that going gay can make one a poet, though the pain of unfulfilment sometimes can.) There came about a deepening willingness to value individual experience in its uniqueness; poets' relationships with women as well as men became more individualised. Donne thinks his mistress is an angel - and then thinks better of it. "It could not choose but be profane, to think thee anything but thee".

Donne has an irreducibly sexist ideology, surely of ecclesiastical not New Testament origin, when he says that men's love is purer than women's.

Shakespeare's cast of mind, it can be claimed, was in no way ideological; men and women in his plays are individuals, in defiance of the then current critical dogma that plays should be populated by types. Malvolio "the ill-wisher" is named straight out of comedy of manners, yet for the rest of time he is his unique self complaining of obstruction to the blood from his cross-gartering. Modern reductive thought generally labels types of love and lovers by gender, but a genuinely religious culture does not classify souls reductively. Marlowe is assumed to have been gay, yet in *Hero and Leander* (Sestiad II 291ff) he wrote this marvellous account of a girl's first love-making:

> She trembling strove, that strife of hers, like that
> Which made the world, another world begat
> Of unknown joy.

Shakespeare's empathetic imagination gave Lear's virtual paederasty its incomparable dream-life in a gilded cage with Cordelia. Of course as a playwright he features promiscuity as the flip side of faithfulness - bawdry was obligatory in the theatre, and often seems no more than 'sex in the head'; yet often he reminds of Terence's credo "nothing about human life is alien to me", as in the highly ingenious couplet (*L.L.L.* 3. i.192)

> A woman, that is like a German clock,
> Still a-repairing, ever out of frame.

He knows better here than in Q20 that moon-like changeability is physiological not a character defect.

The philosopher David Hume claimed to be able to disbelieve in the unity of the self, the continuity through successive moments of individual personality. This is a key belief for Shakespeare. As early as *King John* when Hubert cannot bring himself to blind the child, the child says "Oh now you look like Hubert: all this while You were disguised". Loss of this belief is the madness that dehumanises Troilus. "This is and is not Cressid." "What's her name Since she was Cleopatra?" says Antony. Hamlet cannot bear it that Gertrude does not seem aware of the difference between Claudius and his brother. If you meet your wife in the street and she gives you a blank stare of non-recognition, you will think that either you or she has gone mad. So when sonnets connecting the onset of madness with mistakes about personal identity turn up in Series II, they are likely to be of structural importance, especially for a playwright who based entire plots on such mistaking. And Spenser's *Faery Queen* had made it a template of allegorical thinking as well as of story-line. Series II's whore is a Duessa (false religion) seen as Una (true religion), and that is how the brutality of confusing the friend with her can soften into seeing him as a fellow victim.

The deeply hurtful change of refusing eye contact (Q49.6, cf. Q139.6) could possibly have been a sign of grace in H.W. - it must have been difficult to fall out of love with so rich a personality. In canto 65 of *Avisa* H.W. argues that his wish for phoenix love is real love and not lust, but Semper Eadem (the Queen's phoenix soubriquet translated as 'Alway the same') is relentless. The preface to a later edition says that "some when they have read this book have blushed to themselves finding as they thought their very words and writings". One may speculate however idly whether the real man did plead with the real Queen for his cross-class friendship. Possible hints in the Sonnets of pressure from high quarters are "spies" (Q121) and "suborn'd informer" (Q125). *Avisa* must have been of composite authorship, for long stretches of it are just moronically repetitive doggerel, yet its basic idea is witty, that of wooing "Chastity Herself", since success in that enterprise would be bound to be failure. Chapman's poem also seems to see the Queen as wronged by the defection of a nymph who was to have symbolised a cult of chastity but has somehow mutated into a Calydonian boar, the one that slew Adonis, and is rampaging through the homes of the great. The earl's final encounter with the Queen has been told on p. ix.

The plot that both men woo the same woman is certainly allegorical in *Avisa*. The same plot in the Sonnets has constantly been taken as realistic, but the likelihood of that is minuscule. Sexual rivalry was a duelling matter, and you only duelled with your social equals. Since at least 50 per cent of a British population are dark, the lady cannot be identified by that, and in one mood of the poet's "In nothing art thou black save in thy deeds" (Q131). If you love somone dark you love their darkness, you do not complain of it; the mistress is at best a cautionary tale, not an individual. Nigra and Nigrina can mean a whore in Elizabethan texts, and there is the same colour prejudice in Italian Renaissance usage, possibly derived ultimately from the black horse of the *Phaedrus*. In Q20 the friend was "master mistress", feminine in beauty of face but masculine in character. In Series II he has begun behaving like a woman deceiving her husband, a metaphor which seems to last through three sonnets Qs 93, 140, 139; the latter two must be addressed to the friend because the mad libel in Qs 140 & 147 will be to call him black, which is not a libel on the lady but literal. If he is fickle, evasive and promiscuous he deserves to be mistaken for the sex he despises, to lose his self-image as a Sun King. Q88 had promised an offsetting story of the poet's own faults in his absence after the Farewell. "Since I left you" (Q113) cannot be in place in the section about return to the friend where the Quarto places it. In its thought-mate Q114 loneliness poisons his eyes until in Q148 they "mistake my view". Q148 must be transitional between the two loves, not addressed univocally to the lady as in the Quarto; it cannot be the mistaken love that has worn out his eyes with weeping if their worn out state is what causes them to mistake.

Only terminal placing of the forgiveness section of Series II can resolve the contradictions listed on p. xi. But it seems clear that mutual forgiveness did not happen in the historical relationship. Series II was not presented to its addressee, Q122 makes that clear; and see pp xxv-xxvi on bitter allusions in the plays from the end of 1594 on. Southampton is said to have given Shakespeare a thousand pounds, either as a golden handshake or perhaps an investment in the building of the Globe Theatre. When James I released him from three years in the Tower and he returned to public life and high royal favour, one of the first things he did was to mount a performance of *Love's Labours Lost* in his London home. It must have brought back memories of the halcyon sunshine days of Q33. It was by now a published play, though the first three acts seem abbreviated; perhaps Southampton possessed a fuller text. Did he whisper to his monarch "I was the French Princess when we acted this among ourselves; I had no beard at that age." (This could be the explanation of the Clandon portrait which has been tendentiously described as H.W. "in drag": acting female parts was a male monopoly then, and anyone of his social standing had no need to advertise his bisexuality like a rent-boy). There is sadly no hint of renewed contact with Shakespeare over this production. He had his proper pride, he could hardly have acted in it, or attended not as the author but in the scarlet livery of the King's Men. "A' could never abide carnation" says the Hostess of Falstaff, " 'twas a colour he never liked". At the time he was writing the bitterest of all his plays, *Timon of Athens*. Timon finally commits suicide. Yet even this play ends in the sanity of genius: Alcibiades repudiates Timon's "general and exceptless rashness".

In the closing group of sonnets, Qs.110-111 imply that he did not want to go back to the stage; it is a mercy for world literature that his destiny prevailed over his happiness.

IV *Why has a wrongly paged text been accepted for 400 years?*

Shakespeare outlived its publication by seven years, and would presumably have gone on record as protesting if his text had been tampered with.

Yet an imperfectly lucid text has been much easier for the Zeitgeist of these intervening centuries to come to terms with.

As it happens, the second of these considerations answers the first. Publication had to take account of the biographical level of meaning in preference to the allegorical ones, and of social and moral conventions. It is highly plausible that Shakespeare disordered his text himself, because the true-life element in the story did not end in mutual forgiveness, and because the confusion of high-born friend with whore was libellous however brilliantly psychoanalysed in terms of there being no alternative to love's heaven but the hell of lust without love. The published text is bitter enough in all conscience, leaving him in the toils of a woman who could not tell one possessor of will (name or organ) from another, but it is a more abject ending than the re-paged text's heroic conquest of his Troilus mood, as well as contrary to the common-sense logic set out on this book's p. xi.

These four centuries have lost the limited tolerance of Greek homosexuality which came with the Renaissance. The British law against it was only repealed in 1967, and our national poet is expected to be like Caesar's wife above suspicion. Men of the world whether or not with their fingers crossed have been content to take the message of the Sonnets as summarised by the last line of sonnet 20, even though the sequence shows this formula almost immediately breaking down -

"Mine be thy love, and thy love's use their treasure" (Q20.14).

"Their" in the context means women's, and 'love's use' means sex. Sex is for sharing with women, real affection can be reserved for sharing with other men. Yet the Dark Lady sonnets substitute the terms "abuse" and "misuse" (in Q134.12 and Q152.7) for "love's use" because the relationship is not one of love. English misogyny has revelled in these sonnets yet has managed to believe that they were addressed to an individual woman. Traditional misogyny is generic, and that is much less offensive: - Jacques, "Who can say that I mean her, When such a one as she, such is her neighbour?" (*A.Y.L.* I II 7.78). Most of the railing by angry lovers in the plays is against women who in fact turn out to be loving and innocent. Even to Cressida, the playwright unlike Troilus shows so much humane understanding that he lets her warn Troilus she is not the kind of person who will be faithful: "I have a kind of self resides with you, But an unkind self, that its self will leave To be another's fool". If the author himself seems to hate Helen, that is because of her lethal potential: "For every false drop in her bawdy veins A Grecian life has sunk." He admires Paulina's courage and equalitarianism. Emilia in *Othello* admits infidelity, is then given a splendid outburst against the double moral standard and a heroically brave death. Shakespeare was no misogynist; he had far too strong a sense of individuality, of the difference between one person and another. He had a strong sympathy and sense of justice towards women, e.g. Portia "Your wife would give you little thanks for that" when she hears Antonio say he prefers Bassanio to anyone else (*M. of V.* 4.i.288). He knows Cleopatra's chaotic emotions are not faked; after her rage and desolation at Antony's remarriage, she is helped from the scene saying "Pity me, Charmian, but do not speak to me". He finds the perfect line for a girl of thirteen overwhelmed by a young man: "I have forgot why I did call thee back."

When the life histories of the two genders differ very widely, as they have done during most of these four centuries, the formula that ends Q20 may seem the best available compromise, and wishful thinking may gladly ascribe it to our national poet. Only in the last few decades has the quality of feeling which there can be in same-gender affection become extendable to a female colleague, as it plainly was by the spontaneous outcry of regret when Betty Boothroyd announced her resignation as Speaker of the House of Commons. Many of us know families where that quality of unpossessive warmth is felt by a father for his son, whether child or adult, more than for any other family member. It may even be a factor in the continuing antipathy to gay love, that the element of an ego-trip is perhaps felt to be inseparable from sex and must spoil that unpossessive affection. Our sex-mad culture needs to stop assuming that all lifelong or close friendships are homosexual. A woman who has suffered that misjudgement has been heard to say "The great thing about loving one's own gender is that one can feel their sex organs are their least interesting aspect". A heterosexual model can be felt to be too unequal for friendship, being based on difference not on likeness. There was a short-lived movement at the end of the twentieth century which called itself 'the new celibacy', and produced one or two fine French films; possibly it can claim Antonioni, though he is always cryptic. But the moral responsibility of a literary scholar is not to any particular code or values but to tell the truth as one sees it about texts and their authors.

For centuries our culture has preferred not to understand the Sonnets too closely, and a disordered text makes that much easier, though the order has often been felt to be wrong. The many different attempts to improve it do not indicate that that is a vain endeavour, any more than many different attempts to solve a chess problem prove that there is no solution. Re-paging is the only type of textual emendation which can claim an end-limit of certainty. A little book of card games owned by this editor has had two leaves swapped over in the printing, so that the instructions for several games suddenly make nonsense; exchange the two leaves and all the instructions make perfect sense. Of course no such claim could be made about the complex sense-links that are in question in the Sonnets, but if there are *any* sense-links, permutation arithmetic ceases to be relevant, or one could not solve a jigsaw puzzle. And nonsense-links, like the cart-before-the-horse aspects of the Sonnet's plot in the Quarto text, are a category of sense links. When Rollins in his famous Variorum edition of the Sonnets says that their order is probably wrong but we shall never find the right one, he is not being logical, because every criterion of a wrong conjunction will also serve as a criterion of a right one, or at the least serve to bring a right text nearer.

1609-2009

"Four hundred winters
Thought he not too long"

(with apologies to the carol
"Adam lay ybounden")

In conclusion, there may have emerged from the stages of this introduction an inference which I have been slow to formulate, that Shakespeare in all likelihood copied the plot of Series Two of the Sonnets from the plot of *Willobie His Avisa*, which he will have confronted in the summer of 1594 if not in ms. or by hearsay earlier. He is saying in effect, it was a far far better thing that we should both woo the phoenix, which *Avisa*, deplored, than that we should both woo the loathly lady who is lust unhallowed by any element of beauty or affection. The claim of phoenix love to be chaste is doubtless seen in this light by Ben Jonson, whom no-one suspects of having been gay, when he complains of the "vicious fool" who could well be *Avisa*'s main author:

> But soft: I hear
> Some vicious fool draw near
> That cried we dream; and swears there's no such thing
> As this chaste love we sing.

>> (from *Epos*, published along with Shakespeare's
>> *The Phoenix and the Turtle* in the postlude by leading poets
>> to Chester's *Love's Martyr*)

Does a morality emerge which most thinking and caring people among Shakespeare's readers could subscribe to? Surely that a love which is individual and faithful is better than a generic love (for whichever gender) that readily becomes promiscuous.

Selected passages from the plays - see overleaf

Summary of other references to the plays

Ant.
xviii   xxii

A.Y.L.I.
xxi

Caes.
180   ?misquoted by Ben Jonson

Cor.
175-6

Cym.
xvii   177

Ed. III
171

Ham.
vii   xii   xviii   175   176

Hen. V
xvi   xx   175

2 Hen. VI
xiii   xv

3 Hen. VI
xiv

John
xviii

Lear
xviii   175

L.L.L.
vii   ix   xv   xxiii

M.M.
ix   180

Mer.V.
xxii   180

M.N.D.
vii   ix

Oth.
xxii and see on Q107

Ric. II
175

R.&J.
vii   xxii   180

Tim.
x   xx

Troil.
viii   xxii   179   180

Tw.N.
xxii and see Q96

Wint.
xxii

Selected passages from the plays relevant to betrayed friendship

I Henry IV	2.iv.464 Hal divorces Falstaff in the language of the marriage service: "I will. I do."
II Henry IV	5.iv.48 Falstaff in the coronation procession expects to be greeted with esteem. Hal "I know thee not, old man." Falstaff with great courage merely says he has lost his bet: "Master Shallow, I owe you a thousand pounds."
Henry V	Act II Scenes i and iii The Hostess says "The King hath killed his heart." Falstaff's death is described in terms borrowed from the death of Socrates. Fall-staff is analogous to Shake-spear.
Twelfth Night V. I. 89	Antonio (in an instance of mistaken identity) takes Viola for Sebastian and says:- His false cunning Not meaning to partake with me in danger Taught him to face me out of his acquaintance And grew a twenty years removéd thing Whiles one would wink.

The "danger" was punishment for having captured a ship called the *Phoenix*.

II ii 27	Note Viola's compassion for same-sex love: "Poor lady, she were better love a dream".
A.Y.L.I. II vii 176	Blow, blow thou winter wind Thou art not so unkind As man's ingratitude . . . Thy sting is not so sharp As friends remembered not . . . Most friendship is feigning . . .

III 3.165

> For Time is like a fashionable host
> That slightly shakes his parting guest by the hand
> And with his arms outstretched as he would fly
> Grasps in the comer.

> There is contempt in the 'camp' portrayal of Achilles
> and Patroclus, but only Patroclus' death brings
> Archilles raging back into the battle.

Hamlet and *Timon of Athens* are relevant as whole plays.

Earlier References

It is difficult to date the Introduction to the *Shrew*, but the mocking of Timothy Sly by thc Lord docs sccm rclcvant. Hc is offcrcd luxurics, and a pagc for a bcd-mate, but all he really wants is "a very small beer." Bottom in *M.N.D.* has luxuries pressed on him and services which he cannot think how to use. *M.N.D.* was probably acted in the last month of 1594 by the old calendar (in modern dating February 1595) for the wedding of Lord Burleigh's grand-daughter whom H.W. had refused to marry. Hence the daring and bitter parody of H.W. as Titania briefly in love with an ass of an actor. The play refers to the freakishly bad summer of 1594. Shakespeare rejoined an acting company in late 1594. As for *Love's Labours Lost,* the possibility mooted on p. xx, that the Clandon portrait of H.W. represents him acting the French Princess, calls for a radical reinterpretation of the play.

A valuable book of which this edition has made much use is G.P.V. Akrigg's *Shakespeare and the Earl of Southampton* (Hamish Hamilton). It has a chapter which makes a quite different selection from this of relevant passages from the plays.

The Phoenix and the Turtle

"how hard true sorrow hits" (Q120)

Shakespeare's Sonnets are a tragedy, the story of a personal relationship which failed. That can surely be felt by people of all sympathies, from those who would blame the failure on its sexual unorthodoxy to those who accuse orthodoxy of prejudice.

The greater man was very hard hit, as shown by the recurrent bitter references to betrayed friendship in the plays. Yet he benefited enormously in his work; he picked up a wide-ranging higher education from highly cultured company, in comedy he kept the joyous playfulness of people who have once been very happy together, in history and tragedy he could show with convincing naturalness how people at the top of society behave and talk and think, and that they are always first and foremost real human beings.

Shakespeare's colleague in Southampton's service Florio translated Montaigne's essay on friendship, and one third of Shakespeare's poem *The Phoenix and the Turtle*, six verses, is a close paraphrase of Florio, whose prose climax he leaves to speak for itself: "If I am asked why I loved him, I can only say, Because it was he, because it was myself." That some scholars have thought or said they thought this poem is about the death of a Queen who was not yet dead (high treason surely?) shows what obstacles there are to objectivity in this context.

Both friends knew the Platonic ideal which the phoenix symbolised for the Elizabethans, though it was a bivalent symbol aware of Greek customs as well as of Plato's idealism. Shakespeare lamented at the end of his poem that the ideal was dead.

> Beauty, truth and rarity,
> Grace in all simplicity,
> Here enclos'd in cinders lie . . .
>
> Truth may seem, but cannot be,
> Beauty brag, but tis not she:
> Truth and beauty buried be.
>
> To this urn let those repair
> Who are either true or fair,
> For these dead birds sigh a prayer.

TO.THE.ONLIE.BEGETTER.OF.
THESE.INSVNG.SONNETS.
Mr.W.H. ALL.HAPPINESSE.
AND.THAT.ETERNITIE.
PROMISED.
BY.
OVR.EVER-LIVING.POET.
WISHETH.
THE.WELL-WISHING.
ADVENTVRER.IN.
SETTING.
FORTH.

T.T.

This is the published dedication not the notebook's,
but "onlie begetter" must be Shakespeare's phrase.
See longer notes.

SERIES ONE

Q1

From fairest creatures we desire increase,
That thereby beauty's Rose might never die,
But as the riper should by time decease,
His tender heir might bear his memory:
But thou contracted to thine own bright eyes
Feed'st thy light's flame with self-substantial fuel,
Making a famine where abundance lies,
Thy self thy foe, to thy sweet self too cruel:
Thou that art now the world's fresh ornament
And only herald to the gaudy spring
Within thine own bud buriest thy content,
And tender churl mak'st waste in niggarding:
Pity the world, or else this glutton be
To eat the world's due by the grave and thee.

Lefthand paging of the first Sonnet in the notebook so as
not to waste the verso of the dedication brings nearly all
closely linked Sonnets onto facing pages.

Symbols used in the text, top right hand corners

R = reversed leaf (see p. 167)
T = transposed section of text

Q2

When forty winters shall besiege thy brow
And dig deep trenches in thy beauty's field,
Thy youth's proud livery so gaz'd on now
Will be a tatter'd weed of small worth held:
Then being ask'd, where all thy beauty lies,
Where all the treasure of thy lusty days,
To say, within thine own deep sunken eyes,
Were an all-eating shame, and thriftless praise.
How much more praise deserved thy beauty's use,
If thou couldst answer, this fair child of mine
Shall sum my count and make my eld excuse,
Proving his beauty by succession thine.
This were to be new made when thou art old
And see thy blood warm when thou feel'st it cold.

Lines 10 to 12 illustrate the difficulty of punctuating
these poems, by shifting in mid-sentence from direct
to indirect speech.

Q3

Look in thy glass and tell the face thou viewest
Now is the time that face should form an other,
Whose fresh repair if now thou not renewest,
Thou dost beguile the world, unbless some mother.
For where is she so fair whose unear'd womb
Disdains the tillage of thy husbandry?
Or who is he so fond will be the tomb
Of his self-love, to stop posterity?
Thou art thy mother's glass and she in thee
Calls back the lovely April of her prime,
So thou through windows of thine age shalt see
Despite of wrinkles this thy golden time.
But if thou live remember'd not to be,
Die single and thine image dies with thee.

Line 9: See the extant portraits.

Q4

Unthrifty loveliness, why dost thou spend
Upon thy self thy beauty's legacy?
Nature's bequest gives nothing but doth lend,
And being frank she lends to those are free:
Then beauteous niggard why dost thou abuse
The bounteous largess given thee to give?
Profitless usurer why dost thou use
So great a sum of sums yet canst not live?
For having traffic with thy self alone
Thou of thy self thy sweet self dost deceive,
Then how when nature calls thee to be gone,
What acceptable audit canst thou leave?
Thy unus'd beauty must be tomb'd with thee,
Which uséd lives the executor to be.

Q5

Those hours that with gentle work did frame
The lovely gaze where every eye doth dwell
Will play the tyrants to the very same,
And that un-fair which fairly doth excel:
For never-resting time leads summer on
To hideous winter and confounds him there,
Sap check'd with frost and lusty leaves quite gone,
Beauty o'er-snow'd and bareness everywhere:
Then were not summer's distillation left
A liquid prisoner pent in walls of glass,
Beauty's effect with beauty were bereft,
Nor it nor no remembrance what it was.
But flowers distill'd, though they with winter meet,
Leese but their show, their substance still lives sweet.

Q6

Then let not winter's ragged hand deface
In thee thy summer ere thou be distill'd:
Make sweet some vial; treasure thou some place
With beauty's treasure ere it be self-kill'd:
That use is not forbidden usury
Which happies those that pay the willing loan;
That's for thy self to breed an other thee,
Or ten times happier be it ten for one;
Ten times thy self were happier than thou art
If ten of thine ten times refigur'd thee,
Then what could death do if thou shouldst depart
Leaving thee living in posterity?
Be not self-will'd for thou art much too fair
To be death's conquest and make worms thine heir.

The connection of thought across the open page is
pointed out by the word "Then".

Q7

Lo in the Orient when the gracious light
Lifts up his burning head, each under eye
Doth homage to his new appearing sight,
Serving with looks his sacred majesty,
And having climb'd the steep-up heavenly hill,
Resembling strong youth in his middle age,
Yet mortal looks adore his beauty still,
Attending on his golden pilgrimage:
But when from highmost pitch with weary car
Like feeble age he reeleth from the day,
The eyes (fore duteous) now converted are
From his low tract, and look an other way:
So thou, thy self outgoing in thy noon:
Unlook'd on diest unless thou get a son.

The sun comparison is important and will recur.
He is not just a private person.

Q8

Music to hear, why hear'st thou music sadly?
Sweets with sweets war not, joy delights in joy:
Why lov'st thou that which thou receiv'st not gladly,
Or else receiv'st with pleasure thine annoy?
If the true concord of well tuned sounds
By unions married do offend thine ear,
They do but sweetly chide thee, who confounds
In singleness the parts that thou shouldst bear:
Mark how one string, sweet husband to an other,
Strikes each in each by mutual ordering;
Resembling sire, and child, and happy mother,
Who all in one, one pleasing note do sing:
Whose speechless song being many, seeming one,
Sings this to thee: thou single wilt prove none.

Compare *M. of V.* v.1 69 "I am never merry when
I hear sweet Music".

Q9

Is it for fear to wet a widow's eye
That thou consum'st thy self in single life?
Ah, if thou issueless shalt hap to die,
The world will wail thee like a makeless wife,
The world will be thy widow and still weep
That thou no form of thee hast left behind,
When every private widow well may keep,
By children's eyes, her husband's shape in mind:
Look what an unthrift in the world doth spend
Shifts but his place, for still the world enjoys it,
But beauty's waste hath in the world an end,
And kept unus'd the user so destroys it:
No love toward others in that bosom sits
That on himself such murderous shame commits.

The world-soul values the ideal beloved, as elsewhere
e.g. Qs 106-8.

Q10

For shame, deny that thou bear'st love to any
Who for thy self art so unprovident;
Grant if thou wilt, thou art belov'd of many,
But that thou none lov'st is most evident:
For thou art so possess'd with murderous hate
That gainst thy self thou stick'st not to conspire,
Seeking that beauteous roof to ruinate
Which to repair should be thy chief desire:
O change thy thought, that I may change my mind,
Shall hate be fairer lodg'd than gentle love?
Be as thy presence is gracious and kind,
Or to thy self at least kind-hearted prove,
Make thee an other self for love of me,
That beauty still may live in thine or thee.

The implications of Qs 9-10 are discussed in the Introduction p. viii.
Line 7 See p. xvi on the repairs needed by Beaulieu Abbey.

Q11

As fast as thou shalt wane so fast thou grow'st,
In one of thine, from that which thou departest,
And that fresh blood which youngly thou bestow'st
Thou mayst call thine, when thou from youth convertest;
Herein lives wisdom, beauty, and increase,
Without this, folly, age, and cold decay,
If all were minded so, the times should cease,
And threescore year would make the world away:
Let those whom nature hath not made for store,
Harsh, featureless, and rude, barrenly perish;
Look whom she best endow'd, she gave thee more,
Which bounteous gift thou shouldst in bounty cherish;
She carv'd thee for her seal, and meant thereby
Thou shouldst print more, not let that copy die.

Q12

When I do count the clock that tells the time,
And see the brave day sunk in hideous night,
When I behold the violet past prime,
And sable curls o'ersilver'd o'er with white:
When lofty trees I see barren of leaves
Which erst from heat did canopy the herd
And summer's green all girded up in sheaves
Bornc on the bier with white and bristly beard:
Then of thy beauty do I question make
That thou among the wastes of time must go,
Since sweets and beauties do themselves forsake,
And die as fast as they see others grow,
And nothing gainst Time's scythe can make defence
Save breed to brave him when he takes thee hence.

Q13

O that you were your self, but love you are
No longer yours than you your self here live;
Against this coming end you should prepare,
And your sweet semblance to some other give.
So should that beauty which you hold in lease
Find no determination, then you were
Your self again after your self's decease,
When your sweet issue your sweet form should bear.
Who lets so fair a house fall to decay,
Which husbandry in honour might uphold
Against the stormy gusts of winter's day
And barren rage of death's eternal cold?
O none but unthrifts, dear my love you know
You had a Father, let your Son say so.

'You' instead of 'thou' is for euphony, cf. Q15 "you most
rich in youth", Q54 "And so of you, beauteous and
lovely youth".

Q14

Not from the stars do I my judgment pluck,
And yet methinks I have Astronomy,
But not to tell of good or evil luck,
Of plagues, of dearths, or seasons' quality,
Nor can I fortune to brief minutes tell,
Pointing to each his thunder, rain and wind,
Or say with Princes if it shall go well
By oft predict that I in heaven find.
But from thine eyes my knowledge I derive,
And constant stars, in them I read such art
As truth and beauty shall together thrive
If from thy self to store thou wouldst convert:
Or else of thee this I prognosticate,
Thy end is Truth's and Beauty's doom and date.

Q15

When I consider every thing that grows
Holds in perfection but a little moment:
That this huge stage presenteth nought but shows
Whereon the stars in secret influence comment:
When I perceive that men as plants increase,
Cheered and check'd even by the selfsame sky:
Vaunt in their youthful sap, at height decrease,
And wear their brave state out of memory:
Then the conceit of this inconstant stay
Sets you most rich in youth before my sight,
Where wasteful time debateth with decay
To change your day of youth to sullied night,
And all in war with Time for love of you
As he takes from you, I engraft you new.

Q16

But wherefore do not you a mightier way
Make war upon this bloody tyrant time?
And fortify your self in your decay
With means more blessed than my barren rhyme?
Now stand you on the top of happy hours,
And many maiden gardens yet unset
With virtuous wish would bear your living flowers,
Much liker than your painted counterfeit:
So should the lines of life that life repair
Which this Time's pencil or my pupil pen
Neither in inward worth nor outward fair
Can make you live your self in eyes of men.
To give away your self keeps your self still,
And you must live drawn by your own sweet skill.

Line 10 cf. The Hilliard miniature on p. vi.
H.W. had no beard up to about age 19.

Q17

Who will believe my verse in time to come
If it were fill'd with your most high deserts?
Though yet heaven knows it is but as a tomb
Which hides your life, and shows not half your parts:
If I could write the beauty of your eyes
And in fresh numbers number all your graces
The age to come would say, this Poet lies,
Such heavenly touches ne'er touch'd earthly faces.
So should my papers (yellowed with their age)
Be scorn'd, like old men of less truth than tongue,
And your true rights be term'd a Poet's rage
And stretched metre of an antique song.
But were some child of yours alive that time,
You should live twice, in it, and in my rhyme.

Q18

Shall I compare thee to a Summer's day?
Thou art more lovely and more temperate:
Rough winds do shake the darling buds of May
And Summer's lease hath all too short a date:
Sometime too hot the eye of heaven shines
And often is his gold complexion dimm'd'
And every fair from fair sometime declines,
By chance or nature's changing course untrimm'd:
But thy eternal Summer shall not fade
Nor lose possession of that fair thou ow'st,
Nor shall death brag thou wander'st in his shade,
When in eternal lines to time thou grow'st;
So long as men can breathe or eyes can see,
So long lives this, and this gives life to thee.

Line 1 is not just a rhetorical question but pursues Q17's wish
to convince posterity. The end is not just a boast - Bacon,
"books [are] . . . exempted from the wrong of time".
Line 8 trimming a boat was even more necessary on
Southampton Water than on the Avon.

Q19

Devouring time, blunt thou the Lion's paws
And make the earth devour her own sweet brood,
Pluck the keen teeth from the fierce Tiger's jaws
And burn the long-liv'd Phoenix in her blood,
Make glad and sorry seasons as thou fleet'st
And do whate'er thou wilt, swift-footed time,
To the wide world and all her fading sweets:
But I forbid thee one most heinous crime,
O carve not with thy hours my love's fair brow
Nor draw no lines there with thine antique pen,
Him in thy course untainted do allow
For beauty's pattern to succeeding men.
Yet do thy worst, old Time, despite thy wrong
My love shall in my verse ever live young.

R

Q55
Not marble, nor the gilded monument
Of Princes shall outlive this powerful rhyme,
But you shall shine more bright in these contents
Than unswept stone, besmear'd with sluttish time.
When wasteful war shall statues overturn
And broils root out the work of masonry,
Nor Mars his sword, nor war's quick fire shall burn
The living record of your memory.
Gainst death, and all-oblivious enmity
Shall you pace forth, your praise shall still find room
Even in the eyes of all posterity
That wear this world out to the ending doom.
So till the judgment that your self arise
You live in this, and dwell in lovers' eyes.

Q54

Oh how much more doth beauty beauteous seem
By that sweet ornament which truth doth give;
The Rose looks fair, but fairer we it deem
For that sweet odour which doth in it live:
The Canker blooms have full as deep a dye
As the perfumed tincture of the Roses,
Hang on such thorns, and play as wantonly
When summer's breath their masked buds discloses:
But for their virtue only is their show
They live unwoo'd, and unrespected fade,
Die to themselves. Sweet Roses do not so,
Of their sweet deaths are sweetest odours made:
And so of you, beauteous and lovely youth,
When that shall vade, by verse distils your truth.

New subject-matter takes over: truth defies time better
than beauty Canker will later stand for moral faults (the poet
becomes also a father-figure).

Q20

A woman's face with nature's own hand painted
Hast thou the Master Mistress of my passion,
A woman's gentle heart but not acquainted
With shifting change as is false women's fashion,
An eye more bright than theirs, less false in rolling:
Gilding the object whereupon it gazeth,
A man in hue all hues in his controlling,
Which steals men's eyes and women's souls amazeth.
And for a woman wert thou first created,
Till nature as she wrought thee fell a-doting,
And by addition me of thee defeated,
By adding one thing to my purpose nothing.
But since she prick'd thee out for women's pleasure,
Mine be thy love and thy love's use their treasure.

See longer notes.

Q21

So is it not with me as with that Muse
Stirr'd by a painted beauty to his verse,
Who heaven itself for ornament doth use,
And every fair with his fair doth rehearse,
Making a couplement of proud compare
With Sun and Moon, with earth and sea's rich gems:
With April's first-born flowers and all things rare
That heaven's air in this huge rondure hems:
O let me true in love but truly write,
And then believe me, my love is as fair
As any mother's child, though not so bright
As those gold candles fix'd in heaven's air:
Let them say more that like of hearsay well,
I will not praise that purpose not to sell.

Q22

My glass shall not persuade me I am old
So long as youth and thou are of one date,
But when in thee time's furrows I behold
Then look I death my days should expiate.
For all that beauty that doth cover thee
Is but the seemly raiment of my heart,
Which in thy breast doth live, as thine in me,
How can I then be elder than thou art?
O therefore love be of thy self so wary
As I not for my self, but for thee will,
Bearing thy heart which I will keep so chary
As tender nurse her babe from faring ill,
Presume not on thy heart when mine is slain,
Thou gav'st me thine not to give back again.

The couplet implies a permanent commitment, cf. Q25.

Q23

As an unperfect actor on the stage,
Who with his fear is put besides his part,
Or some fierce thing replete with too much rage,
Whose strength's abundance weakens his own heart:
So I, for fear of trust, forget to say
The perfect ceremony of love's right,
And in mine own love's strength seem to decay,
O'er-charg'd with burthen of mine own love's might:
O let my books be then the eloquence
And dumb presagers of my speaking breast,
Who plead for love, and look for recompense
More than that tongue that more hath more express'd.
O learn to read what silent love hath writ,
To hear with eyes belongs to love's fine wit.

See longer notes and p. 178.

Q24

Mine eye hath play'd the painter and hath stell'd
Thy beauty's form in table of my heart,
My body is the frame wherein 'tis held,
And pérspective it is best Painter's art.
For through the Painter must you see his skill
To find where your true Image pictur'd lies,
Which in my bosom's shop is hanging still,
That hath his windows glazed with thine eyes:
Now see what good turn's eyes for eyes have done,
Mine eyes have drawn thy shape, and thine for me
Are windows to my breast, wherethrough the Sun
Delights to peep, to gaze therein on thee.
Yet eyes this cunning want to grace their art,
They draw but what they see, know not the heart.

Pérspective is used as adj. or adverb - "seen in that way".
Meant a glass toy which gave a clear picture from only
one angle.

Q25

Let those who are in favour with their stars
Of public honour and proud titles boast,
Whilst I whom fortune of such triumph bars
Unlook'd for joy in that I honour most;
Great Princes' favourites their fair leaves spread
But as the Marigold at the sun's eye,
And in themselves their pride lies buried,
For at a frown they in their glory die.
The painful warrior famoused for worth,
After a thousand victories once foil'd,
Is from the book of honour razed quite
And all the rest forgot for which he toil'd:
Then happy I that love and am beloved
Where I may not remove, nor be removed.

Lines 9 and 11: The Quarto text does not decide between
two rhyme schemes, worth/forth and might/quite.

Q26

Lord of my love, to whom in vassalage
Thy merit hath my duty strongly knit,
To thee I send this written ambassage
To witness duty, not to show my wit:
Duty so great, which wit so poor as mine
May make seem bare, in wanting words to show it;
But that I hope some good conceit of thine
In thy soul's thought (all naked) will bestow it:
Till whatsoever star that guides my moving
Points on me graciously with fair aspect,
And puts apparel on my tattered loving,
To show me worthy of thy sweet respect;
Then may I dare to boast how I do love thee,
Till then, not show my head where thou mayst prove me.

Seems to present for approval what has been written so far.
Absence whether literal or fictional will permit more personal
emotion.

Q27

Weary with toil, I haste me to my bed,
The dear repose for limbs with travel tired,
But then begins a journey in my head
To work my mind, when body's work's expired.
For then my thoughts (from far where I abide)
Intend a zealous pilgrimage to thee,
And keep my drooping eyelids open wide,
Looking on darkness which the blind do see:
Save that my soul's imaginary sight
Presents thy shadow to my sightless view,
Which like a jewel (hung in ghastly night)
Makes black night beauteous, and her old face new.
Lo thus by day my limbs, by night my mind
For thee, and for my self, no quiet find.

Q28

How can I then return in happy plight
That am debarr'd the benefit of rest?
When day's oppression is not eas'd by night,
But day by night and night by day oppress'd,
And each (though enemies to either's reign)
Do in consent shake hands to torture me,
The one by toil, the other to complain
How far I toil, still farther off from thee.
I tell the Day to please him thou art bright
And dost him grace when clouds do blot the heaven:
So flatter I the swart-complexion'd night
When sparkling stars twire not thou guil'st the even.
But day doth daily draw my sorrows longer,
And night doth nightly make grief's length seem stronger.

Q43

When most I wink then do mine eyes best see,
For all the day they view things unrespected,
But when I sleep, in dreams they look on thee,
And darkly bright, are bright in dark directed.
Then thou whose shadow shadows doth make bright,
How would thy shadow's form form happy show
To the clear day with thy much clearer light,
When to un-seeing eyes thy shade shines so?
How would (I say) mine eyes be blessed made
By looking on thee in the living day,
When in dead night thy fair imperfect shade
Through heavy sleep on sightless eyes doth stay?
All days are nights to see till I see thee,
And nights bright days when dreams do show thee me.

p. 166 explains what could have happened to the
pagination here. Britten set this sonnet in his Nocturne.

Q44

If the dull substance of my flesh were thought,
Injurious distance should not stop my way,
For then despite of space I would be brought,
From limits far remote, where thou dost stay:
No matter then although my foot did stand
Upon the farthest earth remov'd from thee,
For nimble thought can jump both sea and land
As soon as think the place where he would be.
But ah, thought kills me that I am not thought
To leap large lengths of miles when thou art gone,
But that so much of earth and water wrought
I must attend time's leisure with my moan,
Receiving naught by elements so slow
But heavy tears, badges of either's woe.

Q45

The other two, slight air and purging fire,
Are both with thee, wherever I abide,
The first my thought, the other my desire,
These present-absent with swift motion slide.
For when these quicker elements are gone
In tender embassy of love to thee,
My life being made of four, with two alone
Sinks down to death, oppress'd with melancholy:
Until life's composition be recured
By those swift messengers return'd from thee,
Who even but now come back again assured
Of thy fair health, recounting it to me:
This told, I joy, but then no longer glad
I send them back again, and straight grow sad.

Q46

Mine eye and heart are at a mortal war
How to divide the conquest of thy sight,
Mine eye my heart thy picture's sight would bar,
My heart mine eye the freedom of that right;
My heart doth plead that thou in him dost lie
(A closet never pierc'd with crystal eyes)
But the defendant doth that plea deny
And says in him thy fair appearance lies.
To 'cide this title is impaneled
A quest of thoughts, all tenants to the heart,
And by their verdict is determined
The clear eye's moiety and the dear heart's part:
As thus, mine eye's due is thy outward part
And my heart's right thy inward love of heart.

"thy picture" here and in Q47 probably means the Hilliard
miniature (beardless therefore of early 1590s).
Copies of miniatures were made for sale, cf. *Ham*.2.ii.383.

Q47

Betwixt mine eye and heart a league is took,
And each doth good turns now unto the other,
When that mine eye is famish'd for a look,
Or heart in love with sighs himself doth smother;
With my love's picture then my eye doth feast
And to the painted banquet bids my heart:
An other time my eye is my heart's guest
And in his thoughts of love doth share a part.
So either by thy picture or my love
Thy self away art present still with me,
For thou not farther than my thoughts canst move
And I am still with them, and they with thee.
Or if they sleep, thy picture in my sight
Awakes my heart, to heart's and eye's delight.

Q52

So am I as the rich whose blessed key
Can bring him to his sweet up-locked treasure,
The which he will not every hour survey,
For blunting the fine point of seldom pleasure.
Therefore are feasts so solemn and so rare
Since seldom coming, in the long year set
Like stones of worth they thinly placed are,
Or captain Jewels in the carcanet.
So is the time that keeps you as my chest,
Or as the wardrobe which the robe doth hide,
To make some special instant special blest
By new unfolding his imprison'd pride.
Blessed are you whose worthiness gives scope
Being had to triumph, being lack'd to hope.

This must precede Q48 which dynamites the jewel chest
here used as an image of safety and trust. See p. 166.

Q53

What is your substance, whereof are you made,
That millions of strange shadows on you tend?
Since every one hath, every one, one shade,
And you, but one, can every shadow lend:
Describe Adonis and the counterfeit
Is poorly imitated after you,
On Helen's cheek all art of beauty set
And you in Grecian tires are painted new:
Speak of the spring and foison of the year,
The one doth shadow of your beauty show,
The other as your bounty doth appear,
And you in every blessed shape we know.
In all external grace you have some part,
But you like none, none you for constant heart.

See longer notes.

T

Q50

How heavy do I journey on the way,
When what I seek (my weary travel's end)
Doth teach that ease and that repose to say
Thus far the miles are measur'd from thy friend.
The beast that bears me, tired with my woe,
Plods dully on, to bear that weight in me,
As if by some instinct the wretch did know
His rider lov'd not speed being made from thee:
The bloody spur cannot provoke him on
That sometimes anger thrusts into his hide,
Which heavily he answers with a groan
More sharp to me than spurring to his side,
For that same groan doth put this in my mind,
My grief lies onward and my joy behind.

With Q51 the natural pair to end the journey.
Line 14 grimly equivocal.

Q51

Thus can my love excuse the slow offence
Of my dull bearer, when from thee I speed:
From where thou art, why should I haste me thence?
Till I return, of posting is no need.
O what excuse will my poor beast then find
When swift extremity can seem but slow,
Then should I spur though mounted on the wind,
In winged speed no motion shall I know,
Then can no horse with my desire keep pace,
Therefore desire (of perfect'st love being made)
Shall neigh no dull flesh in his fiery race,
But love, for love, thus shall excuse my jade,
Since from thee going he went wilful slow,
Towards thee I'll run, and give him leave to go.

See p. xvii.

T

Q29

When in disgrace with Fortune and men's eyes
I all alone beweep my outcast state,
And trouble deaf heaven with my bootless cries
And look upon my self and curse my fate,
Wishing me like to one more rich in hope,
Featur'd like him, like him with friends possess'd,
Desiring this man's art, and that man's scope,
With what I most enjoy contented least,
Yet in these thoughts my self almost despising
Haply I think on thee, and then my state
Like to the lark at break of day arising
From sullen earth sings hymns at heaven's gate,
For thy sweet love rememb'red such wealth brings
That then I scorn to change my state with kings.

"disgrace" could refer to the "vulgar scandal" (Q112).

Q30

When to the Sessions of sweet silent thought
I summon up remembrance of things past,
I sigh the lack of many a thing I sought
And with old woes new wail my dear time's waste:
Then can I drown an eye (unus'd to flow)
For precious friends hid in death's dateless night,
And weep afresh love's long since cancell'd woe,
And moan the expense of many a vanish'd sight:
Then can I grieve at grievances foregone
And heavily from woe to woe tell o'er
The sad account of fore-bemoaned moan,
Which I new pay as if not paid before.
But if the while I think on thee (dear friend)
All losses are restor'd, and sorrows end.

Could refer to Marlowe's death in 1593, since the future of the unfinished *Hero and Leander* may have been the chief cause of the coming breach (see pp. xiv and 170).

Q31

Thy bosom is endeared with all hearts
Which I by lacking have supposed dead,
And there reigns Love and all Love's loving parts,
And all those friends which I thought buried.
How many a holy and obsequious tear
Hath dear religious love stol'n from mine eye,
As interest of the dead, which now appear
But things remov'd that hidden in there lie.
Thou art the grave where buried love doth live,
Hung with the trophies of my lovers gone,
Who all their parts of me to thee did give,
That due of many now is thine alone.
Their images I lov'd I view in thee,
And thou (all they) hast all the all of me.

Q32

If thou survive my well contented day
When that churl death my bones with dust shall cover,
And shalt by fortune once more re-survey
These poor rude lines of thy deceased Lover:
Compare them with the bettering of the time,
And though they be out-stripp'd by every pen,
Reserve them for my love, not for their rhyme,
Exceeded by the height of happier men.
Oh then vouchsafe me but this loving thought,
Had my friend's Muse grown with this growing age,
A dearer birth than this his love had brought
To march in ranks of better equipage:
But since he died and Poets better prove,
Theirs for their style I'll read, his for his love.

Q33

Full many a glorious morning have I seen
Flatter the mountain tops with sovereign eye,
Kissing with golden face the meadows green,
Gilding pale streams with heavenly alchemy,
Anon permit the basest clouds to ride
With ugly rack on his celestial face,
And from the forlorn world his visage hide
Stealing unseen to west with this disgrace:
Even so my Sun one early morn did shine
With all-triumphant splendour on my brow,
But out alack, he was but one hour mine,
The region cloud hath mask'd him from me now.
Yet him for this my love no whit disdaineth,
Suns of the world may stain, when heaven's sun staineth.

A landmark sonnet, and chief proof of a halcyon period at the start of the friendship.

Q34

Why didst thou promise such a beauteous day,
And make me travel forth without my cloak,
To let base clouds o'ertake me in my way,
Hiding thy bravery in their rotten smoke.
Tis not enough that through the cloud thou break
To dry the rain on my storm-beaten face,
For no man well of such a salve can speak
That heals the wound, and cures not the disgrace:
Nor can thy shame give physic to my grief,
Though thou repent, yet I have still the loss,
The offender's sorrow lends but weak relief
To him that bears the strong offence's cross.
Ah but those tears are pearl which thy love sheds,
And they are rich, and ransom all ill deeds.

Q120 refers back to this scene of shared sorrow.

Q35

No more be griev'd at that which thou hast done,
Roses have thorns, and silver fountains mud,
Clouds and eclipses stain both Moon and Sun,
And loathsome canker lives in sweetest bud.
All men make faults, and even I in this,
Authorising thy trespass with compare,
My self corrupting salving thy amiss,
Excusing thy sins more than thy sins are:
For to thy sensual fault I bring in sense,
Thy adverse party is thy Advocate,
And gainst my self a lawful plea commence,
Such civil war is in my love and hate
That I an accessory needs must be
To that sweet thief which sourly robs from me.

Sets up the Court of Love scene in which alone the
stolen mistress features.

Q36

Let me confess that we two must be twain,
Although our undivided loves are one:
So shall those blots that do with me remain
Without thy help, by me be borne alone.
In our two loves there is but one respect,
Though in our lives a separable spite,
Which though it alter not love's sole effect
Yet doth it steal sweet hours from love's delight,
I may not evermore acknowledge thee
Lest my bewailed guilt should do thee shame,
Nor thou with public kindness honour me
Unless thou take that honour from thy name:
But do not so, I love thee in such sort
As thou being mine, mine is thy good report.

"bewailed guilt" may be ironic, cf. Q49's self-vindication
by means of the apparent opposite. See p. xiv.

Q37

As a decrepit father takes delight
To see his active child do deeds of youth,
So I, made lame by Fortune's dearest spite,
Take all my comfort of thy worth and truth.
For whether beauty, birth, or wealth, or wit,
Or any of these all, or all, or more
Entitled in their parts, do crowned sit,
I make my love engrafted to this store:
So then I am not lame, poor, nor despis'd,
Whilst that this shadow doth such substance give
That I in thy abundance am suffic'd
And by a part of all thy glory live:
Look what is best, that best I wish in thee,
This wish I have, then ten times happy me.

Q38

How can my Muse want subject to invent
While thou dost breathe that pour'st into my verse
Thine own sweet argument, too excellent
For every vulgar paper to rehearse:
Oh give thy self the thanks if aught in me
Worthy perusal stand against thy sight,
For who's so dumb that cannot write to thee,
When thou thy self dost give invention light?
Be thou the tenth Muse, ten times more in worth
Than those old nine which rhymers invocate,
And he that calls on thee, let him bring forth
Eternal numbers to outlive long date.
If my slight Muse do please these curious days,
The pain be mine, but thine shall be the praise.

Poet rivals are uppermost in mind.

Q39

Oh how thy worth with manners may I sing
When thou art all the better part of me?
What can mine own praise to mine own self bring;
And what is't but mine own when I praise thee:
Even for this, let us divided live,
And our dear love lose name of single one,
That by this separation I may give
That due to thee which thou deserv'st alone:
Oh absence what a torment wouldst thou prove,
Were it not thy sour leisure gave sweet leave
To entertain the time with thoughts of love,
Which time and thoughts so sweetly dost deceive,
And that thou teachest how to make one twain,
By praising him here who doth hence remain.

A lawcourt fiction that divides the friend into two and generates
the mistress. But cf, Qs 48-9. self-theft is not a crime, hence
there is "no cause" before the court. Cf. *V. and A*. 160
"Steal thine own freedom and complain on theft".

Q40

Take all my loves, my love, yea take them all,
What hast thou then more than thou hadst before?
No love, my love, that thou mayst true love call,
All mine was thine, before thou hadst this more:
Then if for my love, thou my love receivest,
I cannot blame thee, for my love thou usest,
But yet be blam'd, if thou this self deceivest
By wilful taste of what thy self refusest.
I do forgive thy robbery gentle thief
Although thou steal thee all my poverty:
And yet love knows it is a greater grief
To bear love's wrong, than hate's known injury.
Lascivious grace, in whom all ill well shows,
Kill me with spites yet we must not be foes.

Qs 40-41: These two sonnets seem nearest to implying a real
third person. Perhaps he intended that plot at some stage,
then in Series II saw that a different plot would suit his
purpose better.

Q41

Those pretty wrongs that liberty commits,
When I am sometime absent from thy heart,
Thy beauty, and thy years full well befits,
For still temptation follows where thou art.
Gentle thou art, and therefore to be won,
Beauteous thou art, therefore to be assailed:
And when a woman woos, what woman's son
Will sourly leave her till he have prevailed.
Ay me, but yet thou mightst my seat forbear,
And chide thy beauty, and thy straying youth,
Who lead thee in thy riot even there
Where thou art forc'd to break a twofold truth:
Hers by thy beauty tempting her to thee,
Thine by thy beauty being false to me.

Q42

That thou hast her it is not all my grief,
And yet it may be said I lov'd her dearly,
That she hath thee is of my wailing chief,
A loss in love that touches me more nearly.
Loving offenders thus I will excuse ye,
Thou dost love her, because thou knowst I love her,
And for my sake even so doth she abuse me,
Suffering my friend for my sake to approve her;
If I lose thee, my loss is my love's gain,
And losing her, my friend hath found that loss,
Both find each other, and I lose both twain,
And both for my sake lay on me this cross,
But here's the joy, my friend and I are one,
Sweet flattery, then she loves but me alone.

Line 4: An important preference, see p. xvii.

54

Q48

How careful was I, when I took my way,
Each trifle under truest bars to thrust,
That to my use it might unused stay
From hands of falsehood, in sure wards of trust:
But thou, to whom my jewels trifles are,
Most worthy comfort, now my greatest grief,
Thou best of dearest, and mine only care,
Art left the prey of every vulgar thief.
Thee have I not lock'd up in any chest,
Save where thou art not, though I feel thou art,
Within the gentle closure of my breast,
From whence at pleasure thou mayst come and part,
And even thence thou wilt be stol'n I fear,
For truth proves thievish for a prize so dear.

Qs 48-9 end the Sweet Thief trial. See longer notes and p. 179.

Q49

Against that time (if ever that time come)
When I shall see thee frown on my defects,
Whenas thy love hath cast his utmost sum,
Call'd to that audit by advis'd respects,
Against that time when thou shalt strangely pass
And scarcely greet me with that sun thine eye,
When love converted from the thing it was
Shall reasons find of settled gravity:
Against that time do I ensconce me here
Within the knowledge of mine own desert,
And this my hand against my self uprear
To guard the lawful reasons on thy part,
To leave poor me, thou hast the strength of laws,
Since why to love, I can allege no cause.

See p. xiv.

R

Q76

Why is my verse so barren of new pride?
So far from variation or quick change?
Why with the time do I not glance aside
To new-found methods, and to compounds strange?
Why write I still all one, ever the same,
And keep invention in a noted weed,
That every word doth almost tell my name,
Showing their birth, and where they did proceed?
O know sweet love I always write of you,
And you and love are still my argument:
So all my best is dressing old words new,
Spending again what is already spent:
For as the Sun is daily new and old,
So is my love still telling what is told.

A fresh start, but "I always write of you".

Q75

So are you to my thoughts as food to life,
Or as sweet season'd showers are to the ground;
And for the peace of you I hold such strife
As twixt a miser and his wealth is found:
Now proud as an enjoyer, and anon
Doubting the filching age will steal his treasure,
Now counting best to be with you alone,
Then better'd that the world may see my pleasure,
Sometime all full with feasting on your sight,
And by and by clean starved for a look,
Possessing or pursuing no delight
Save what is had or must from you be took.
Thus do I pine and surfeit day by day,
Or gluttoning on all, or all away.

Q56

Sweet love renew thy force, be it not said
Thy edge should blunter be than appetite,
Which but today by feeding is allay'd,
Tomorrow sharpen'd in his former might.
So love be thou, although today thou fill
Thy hungry eyes, even till they wink with fullness,
Tomorrow see again, and do not kill
The spirit of Love, with a perpetual dullness:
Let this sad interim like the ocean be
Which parts the shore, where two contracted new
Come daily to the banks, that when they see
Return of love, more blest may be the view.
As call it Winter, which being full of care
Makes Summer's welcome thrice more wish'd, more rare.

"This sad interim" seems to imply a hope that the breach in the friendship is only temporary.
Brents Stirling saw the close connection of thought between this and Q75.

Q57

Being your slave what should I do but tend
Upon the hours and times of your desire?
I have no precious time at all to spend,
Nor services to do till you require.
Nor dare I chide the world without end hour
Whilst I (my sovereign) watch the clock for you,
Nor think the bitterness of absence sour
When you have bid your servant once adieu.
Nor dare I question with my jealous thought
Where you may be, or your affairs suppose,
But like a sad slave stay and think of nought
Save where you are, how happy you make those.
So true a fool is love, that in your Will
(Though you do anything) he thinks no ill.

These two poems paradoxically show how far from
slavery the past relationship was. See pp. 178-9.

Q58

That God forbid, that made me first your slave,
I should in thought control your times of pleasure,
Or at your hand the account of hours to crave,
Being your vassal bound to stay your leisure.
Oh let me suffer (being at your beck)
The imprison'd absence of your liberty,
And patience tame to sufferance bide each check
Without accusing you of injury.
Be where you list, your charter is so strong
That you your self may privilege your time
To what you will, to you it doth belong
Your self to pardon of self-doing crime.
I am to wait, though waiting so be hell,
Not blame your pleasure be it ill or well.

Q59

If there be nothing new, but that which is
Hath been before, how are our brains beguil'd
Which labouring for invention bear amiss
The second burthen of a former child!
Oh that record could with a backward look,
Even of five hundred courses of the Sun,
Show me your image in some antique book,
Since mind at first in character was done:
That I might see what the old world could say
To this composed wonder of your frame,
Whether we are mended, or whe'er better they,
Or whether revolution be the same.
Oh sure I am the wits of former days
To subjects worse have given admiring praise.

Five hundred years was the lifespan of the phoenix.
Perhaps such ideals have always had some flaw.

Q60

Like as the waves make towards the pebbled shore,
So do our minutes hasten to their end,
Each changing place with that which goes before,
In sequent toil all forwards do contend.
Nativity once in the main of light
Crawls to maturity, wherewith being crown'd,
Crooked eclipses gainst his glory fight,
And time that gave, doth now his gift confound.
Time doth transfix the flourish set on youth
And delves the parallels in beauty's brow,
Feeds on the rarities of nature's truth,
And nothing stands but for his scythe to mow.
And yet to times in hope, my verse shall stand
Praising thy worth, despite his cruel hand.

Q61

Is it thy will, thy Image should keep open
My heavy eyelids to the weary night?
Dost thou desire my slumbers should be broken,
While shadows like to thee do mock my sight?
Is it thy spirit that thou send'st from thee
So far from home into my deeds to pry,
To find out shames and idle hours in me,
The scope and tenor of thy jealousy?
O no, thy love though much, is not so great,
It is my love that keeps mine eye awake,
Mine own true love that doth my rest defeat,
To play the watchman ever for thy sake.
For thee watch I, whilst thou dost awake elsewhere,
From me far off, with others all too near.

Q62

Sin of self-love possesseth all mine eye,
And all my soul, and all my every part;
And for this sin there is no remedy,
It is so grounded inward in my heart.
Methinks no face so gracious is as mine,
No shape so true, no truth of such account,
And for my self mine own worth do define
As I all other in all worths surmount.
But when my glass shows me my self indeed
Beated and chopp'd with tann'd antiquity,
Mine own self love quite contrary I read:
Self so self-loving were iniquity,
Tis thee (my self) that for my self I praise,
Painting my age with beauty of thy days.

Q63

Against my love shall be as I am now
With time's injurious hand crush'd and o'erworn,
When hours have drain'd his blood and fill'd his brow
With lines and wrinkles, when his youthful morn
Hath travel'd on to Age's steepy night,
And all those beauties whereof now he's King
Are vanishing, or vanish'd out of sight,
Stealing away the treasure of his Spring:
For such a time do I now fortify
Against confounding Age's cruel knife,
That he shall never cut from memory
My sweet love's beauty, though my lover's life.
His beauty shall in these black lines be seen,
And they shall live, and he in them still green.

Q64

When I have seen by time's fell hand defaced
The rich proud cost of outworn buried age,
When sometime lofty towers I see down razed,
And brass eternal slave to mortal rage:
When I have seen the hungry ocean gain
Advantage on the kingdom of the shore,
And the firm soil win of the watery main,
Increasing store with loss, and loss with store:
When I have seen such interchange of state
Or state itself confounded to decay,
Ruin hath taught me thus to ruminate
That Time will come and take my love away.
This thought is as a death which cannot choose
But weep to have that which it fears to lose.

Q65

Since brass, nor stone, nor earth, nor boundless sea,
But sad mortality o'ersways their power,
How with this rage shall beauty hold a plea,
Whose action is no stronger than a flower?
O how shall summer's honey breath hold out
Against the wrackful siege of battering days,
When rocks impregnable are not so stout,
Nor gates of steel so strong, but time decays?
O fearful meditation, where alack
Shall time's best Jewel from time's chest lie hid?
Or what strong hand can hold his swift foot back,
Or who his spoil of beauty can forbid?
O none, unless this miracle have might,
That in black ink my love may still shine bright.

Q66

Tir'd with all these for restful death I cry,
As, to behold desert a beggar born,
And needy Nothing trimm'd in jollity,
And purest faith unhappily forsworn,
And gilded honour shamefully misplac'd,
And maiden virtue rudely strumpeted,
And right perfection wrongfully disgrac'd,
And strength by limping sway disabled,
And art made tongue-tied by authority,
And Folly (Doctor-like) controlling skill,
And simple Truth miscall'd Simplicity,
And captive good attending Captain ill:
Tir'd with all these, from these would I be gone,
Save that to die, I leave my love alone.

For a poem to become a list can be a weakness, but
it suits the expression of disgust to be cumulative as here.

Q67

Ah wherefore with infection should he live,
And with his presence grace impiety,
That sin by him advantage should achieve,
And lace itself with his society?
Why should false painting imitate his cheek,
And steal dead seeing of his living hue?
Why should poor beauty indirectly seek
Roses of shadow, since his Rose is true?
Why should he live now nature bankrupt is,
Beggar'd of blood to blush through lively veins,
For she hath no exchequer now but his,
And prov'd of many, lives upon his gains?
O him she stores, to show what wealth she had
In days long since, before these last so bad.

This and Qs. 69-70 are daringly critical - a reminder that the "scandal" has impugned both of them. For the word-music of this octave see longer notes.

Q68

Thus is his cheek the map of days outworn,
When beauty liv'd and died as flowers do now,
Before these bastard signs of fair were born
Or durst inhabit on a living brow:
Before the golden tresses of the dead,
The right of sepulchres, were shorn away
To live a second life on second head,
Ere beauty's dead fleece made another gay:
In him those holy antique hours are seen,
Without all ornament, itself and true,
Making no summer of an other's green,
Robbing no old to dress his beauty new,
And him as for a map doth Nature store
To show false Art what beauty was of yore.

Q69

Those parts of thee that the world's eye doth view
Want nothing that the thought of hearts can mend:
All tongues (the voice of souls) give thee that due,
Uttering bare truth, even so as foes commend.
Thy outward thus with outward praise is crown'd,
But those same tongues that give thee so thine own
In other accents do this praise confound
By seeing farther than the eye hath shown.
They look into the beauty of thy mind,
And that in guess they measure by thy deeds,
Then churls their thoughts (although their eyes were kind)
To thy fair flower add the rank smell of weeds,
But why thy odour matcheth not thy show,
The soil is this, that thou dost common grow.

So far from compliment that he may perhaps have
given up hope of Series I being accepted? John Clapham's
Narcissus was in some ways offensive, but his employer,
Lord Burleigh, will have taken responsibility for that.

Q70

That thou art blam'd shall not be thy defect,
For slander's mark was ever yet the fair,
The ornament of beauty is suspect,
A Crow that flies in heaven's sweetest air.
So thou be good, slander doth but approve
Thy worth the greater being woo'd of time,
For Canker vice the sweetest buds doth love
And thou present'st a pure unstained prime.
Thou hast pass'd by the ambush of young days,
Either not assail'd, or victor being charg'd,
Yet this thy praise cannot be so thy praise
To tie up envy, evermore cnlarg'd;
If some suspect of ill mask'd not thy show,
Then thou alone kingdoms of hearts shouldst owe.

Q71

No longer mourn for me when I am dead
Than you shall hear the surly sullen bell
Give warning to the world that I am fled
From this vile world with vilest worms to dwell:
Nay if you read this line, remember not
The hand that writ it, for I love you so
That I in your sweet thoughts would be forgot,
If thinking on me then should make you woe.
O if (I say) you look upon this verse
When I perhaps compounded am with clay,
Do not so much as my poor name rehearse;
But let your love even with my life decay.
Lest the wise world should look into your moan,
And mock you with me after I am gone.

Q72

O lest the world should task you to recite
What merit liv'd in me that you should love,
After my death (dear love) forget me quite,
For you in me can nothing worthy prove:
Unless you would devise some virtuous lie
To do more for me than mine own desert,
And hang more praise upon deceased I
Than niggard truth would willingly impart:
O lest your true love may seem false in this,
That you for love speak well of me untrue,
My name be buried where my body is,
And live no more to shame nor me nor you.
For I am sham'd by that which I bring forth,
And so should you, to love things nothing worth.

Q73

That time of year thou mayst in me behold
When yellow leaves, or none, or few do hang
Upon those boughs which shake against the cold,
Bare ruin'd choirs, where late the sweet birds sang.
In me thou seest the twilight of such day
As after Sunset fadeth in the West,
Which by and by black night doth take away,
Death's second self that seals up all in rest.
In me thou seest the glowing of such fire
That on the ashes of his youth doth lie,
As the death-bed whereon it must expire,
Consum'd with that which it was nourish'd by.
This thou perceiv'st, which makes thy love more strong
To love that well, which thou must leave ere long.

Q74

But be contented, when that fell arrest
Without all bail shall carry me away,
My life hath in this line some interest,
Which for memorial still with thee shall stay.
When thou reviewest this, thou dost review
The very part was consecrate to thee,
The earth can have but earth, which is his due,
My spirit is thine the better part of me;
So then thou hast but lost the dregs of life,
The prey of worms, my body being dead,
The coward conquest of a wretch's knife,
Too base of thee to be remembered;
The worth of that, is that which it contains,
And that is this, and this with thee remains.

The repeated "this" goes with presentation of the
half-filled book to its addressee.

Q77

Thy glass will show thee how thy beauties wear,
Thy dial how thy precious minutes waste,
The vacant leaves thy mind's imprint will bear,
And of this book, this learning mayst thou taste:
The wrinkles which thy glass will truly show
Of mouthed graves will give thee memory,
Thou by thy dial's shady stealth mayst know
Time's thievish progress to eternity.
Look what thy memory cannot contain
Commit to these waste blanks, and thou shalt find
Those children nurs'd, deliver'd from thy brain,
To take a new acquaintance of thy mind.
These offices, so oft as thou wilt look,
Shall profit thee, and much enrich thy book.

The first Notebook Sonnet ends Series I. The book was half empty (77 is half of 154 sonnets), and when shown to the patron was returned with a complaint about his poet's silence, i.e. not having filled the whole book.

R

SERIES TWO

Q81

Or I shall live your Epitaph to make,
Or you survive when I in earth am rotten,
From hence your memory death cannot take,
Although in me each part will be forgotten.
Your name from hence immortal life shall have
Though I (once gone) to all the world must die,
The earth can yield me but a common grave
When you entombed in men's eyes shall lie,
Your monument shall be my gentle verse
Which eyes not yet created shall o'er-read,
And tongues to be your being shall rehearse,
When all the breathers of this world are dead,
You still shall live (such virtue hath my pen)
Where breath most breathes, even in the mouths of men.

The end of Series I envisaged that one or other man might die,
not fanciful in a time of plague. The covenant for the Southampton
family monument in Titchfield church was signed in May 1594,
and gives line 8 a double meaning.

79

Q80

O how I faint when I of you do write,
Knowing a better spirit doth use your name,
And in the praise thereof spends all his might
To make me tongue-tied speaking of your fame.
But since your worth (wide as the Ocean is)
The humble as the proudest sail doth bear,
My saucy bark (inferior far to his)
On your broad main doth wilfully appear.
Your shallowest help will hold me up afloat,
Whilst he upon your soundless deep doth ride,
Or being wreck'd I am a worthless boat,
He of tall building, and of goodly pride.
Then if he thrive and I be cast away,
The worst was this, my love was my decay.

The reference could be to Marlowe's *Hero and Leander*.
A discouraged mood supercedes the opening sonnet.
See longer notes.

Q78

So oft have I invok'd thee for my Muse,
And found such fair assistance in my verse,
As every alien pen hath got my use
And under thee their poesie disperse.
Thine eyes, that taught the dumb on high to sing
And heavy ignorance aloft to fly,
Have added feathers to the learned's wing
And given grace a double majesty.
Yet be most proud of that which I compile,
Whose influence is thine, and born of thee;
In others' works thou dost but mend the style
And Arts with thy sweet graces graced be;
But thou art all my art, and dost advance
As high as learning my rude ignorance.

Q79

Whilst I alone did call upon thy aid
My verse alone had all thy gentle grace,
But now my gracious numbers are decay'd
And my sick Muse doth give an other place.
I grant (sweet love) thy lovely argument
Deserves the travail of a worthier pen,
Yet what of thee thy Poet doth invent
He robs thee of, and pays it thee again;
He lends thee virtue, and he stole that word
From thy behaviour, beauty doth he give
And found it in thy cheek: he can afford
No praise to thee, but what in thee doth live.
Then thank him not for that which he doth say,
Since what he owes thee, thou thy self dost pay.

Q82

I grant thou wert not married to my Muse,
And therefore mayst without attaint o'erlook
The dedicated words which writers use
Of their fair subject, blessing every book.
Thou art as fair in knowledge as in hue,
Finding thy worth a limit past my praise,
And therefore art enforc'd to seek anew
Some fresher stamp of the time-bettering days.
And do so love, yet when they have devis'd
What strained touches Rhetoric can lend,
Thou, truly fair, wert truly sympathis'd
In true plain words, by thy true telling friend:
And their gross painting might be better us'd
Where cheeks need blood, in thee it is abus'd.

Makes a distinction between personal and
professional loyalties.

Q83

I never saw that you did painting need,
And therefore to your fair no painting set,
I found (or thought I found) you did exceed
The barren tender of a Poet's debt:
And therefore have I slept in your report,
That you your self being extant well might show
How far a modern quill doth come too short,
Speaking of worth, what worth in you doth grow;
This silence for my sin you did impute,
Which shall be most my glory being dumb,
For I impair not beauty being mute,
When others would give life, and bring a tomb.
There lives more life in one of your fair eyes
Than both your Poets can in praise devise.

Line 9: The complaint of silence is easily understood
since the notebook of commissioned sonnets has been
only half filled.

Q84

Who is it that says most, which can say more
Than this rich praise, that you alone are you,
In whose confine immured is the store
Which should example where your equal grew;
Lean penury within that pen doth dwell
That to his subject lends not some small glory,
But he that writes of you, if he can tell
That you are you, so dignifies his story.
Let him but copy what in you is writ,
Not making worse what nature made so clear,
And such a counterpart shall fame his wit,
Making his style admired everywhere.
You to your beauteous blessings add a curse,
Being fond on praise, which makes your praises worse.

Q85

My tongue-tied Muse in manners holds her still,
While comments of your praise richly compil'd
Reserve their character with golden quill
And precious phrase by all the Muses fil'd.
I think good thoughts, whilst others write good words,
And like unlettered clerk still cry Amen
To every Hymn that able spirit affords
In polish'd form of well refined pen.
Hearing you prais'd, I say 'tis so, 'tis true,
And to the most of praise add something more,
But that is in my thought, whose love to you
Though words come hindmost, holds his rank before;
Then others for the breath of words respect,
Me for my dumb thoughts, speaking in effect.

Line 7 "Hymn" was the title of Chapman's scandal-mongering poem about the Sonnet's friendship published in 1594.

Q86

Was it the proud full sail of his great verse,
Bound for the prize of all too precious you,
That did my ripe thoughts in my brain inhearse,
Making their tomb the womb wherein they grew?
Was it his spirit, by spirits taught to write
Above a mortal pitch, that struck me dead?
No, neither he, nor his compeers by night
Giving him aid, my verse astonished.
He nor that affable familiar ghost
Which nightly gulls him with intelligence
As victors of my silence cannot boast,
I was not sick of any fear from thence.
But when your countenance fill'd up his line,
Then lack'd I matter, that enfeebled mine.

Line 13 implies some form of approval has been shown
to Chapman, hence Farewell follows in Q87.
See longer notes.

Q87

Farewell, thou art too dear for my possessing.
And like enough thou know'st thy estimate,
The charter of thy worth gives thee releasing:
My bonds in thee are all determinate.
For how do I hold thee but by thy granting,
And for that riches where is my deserving?
The cause of this fair gift in me is wanting,
And so my patent back again is swerving.
Thy self thou gav'st, thy own worth then not knowing,
Or me, to whom thou gav'st it, else mistaking,
So thy great gift upon misprision growing
Comes home again, on better judgment making.
Thus have I had thee as a dream doth flatter,
In sleep a King, but waking no such matter.

The disyllabic rhymes lack finality because this is the
start of an Odyssey not the end.

Q88

When thou shalt be dispos'd to set me light,
And place my merit in the eye of scorn,
Upon thy side, against my self I'll fight,
And prove thee virtuous, though thou art forsworn:
With mine own weakness being best acquainted,
Upon thy part I can set down a story
Of faults conceal'd, wherein I am attainted,
That thou in losing me shall win much glory:
And I by this will be a gainer too,
For bending all my loving thoughts on thee,
The injuries that to my self I do,
Doing thee vantage, double vantage me.
Such is my love, to thee I so belong,
That for thy right my self will bear all wrong.

Line 6 promises the coming story of the poet's offsetting offence.

Q89

Say that thou didst forsake me for some fault,
And I will comment upon that offence,
Speak of my lameness, and I straight will halt:
Against thy reasons making no defence.
Thou canst not (love) disgrace me half so ill,
To set a form upon desired change,
As I'll my self disgrace, knowing thy will
I will acquaintance strangle and look strange:
Be absent from thy walks, and in my tongue
Thy sweet beloved name no more shall dwell,
Lest I (too much profane) should do it wrong,
And haply of our old acquaintance tell.
For thee, against my self I'll vow debate,
For I must ne'er love him whom thou dost hate.

Accepts the role of scapegoat with passionate eloquence.

Q90

Then hate me when thou wilt, if ever, now,
Now while the world is bent my deeds to cross,
Join with the spite of fortune, make me bow,
And do not drop in for an after-loss:
Ah do not, when my heart hath scap'd this sorrow,
Come in the rearward of a conquer'd woe,
Give not a windy night a rainy morrow,
To linger out a purpos'd overthrow.
If thou wilt leave me, do not leave me last,
When other petty griefs have done their spite,
But in the onset come, so shall I taste
At first the very worst of fortune's might.
And other strains of woe, which now seem woe,
Compar'd with loss of thee, will not seem so.

Q91

Some glory in their birth, some in their skill,
Some in their wealth, some in their bodies' force,
Some in their garments though new-fangled ill:
Some in their hawks and hounds, some in their horse,
And every humour hath his adjunct pleasure
Wherein it finds a joy above the rest,
But these particulars are not my measure,
All these I better in one general best.
Thy love is better than high birth to me,
Richer than wealth, prouder than garments' cost,
Of more delight than hawks or horses be:
And having thee, of all men's pride I boast.
Wretched in this alone, that thou mayst take
All this away, and me most wretched make.

This derives from a Sappho fragment.

Q92

But do thy worst to steal thy self away,
For term of life thou are assured mine,
And life no longer than thy love will stay,
For it depends upon that love of thine.
Then need I not to fear the worst of wrongs,
When in the least of them my life hath end,
I see a better state to me belongs
Than that which on thy humour doth depend.
Thou canst not vex me with inconstant mind,
Since that my life on thy revolt doth lie,
Oh what a happy title do I find,
Happy to have thy love, happy to die!
But what's so blessed fair that fears no blot,
Thou mayst be false and yet I know it not.

See longer notes on Qs 92-139.

Q93

So shall I live supposing thou art true,
Like a deceived husband, so love's face
May still seem love to me, though alter'd new:
Thy looks with me, thy heart in other place.
For there can live no hatred in thine eye,
Therefore in that I cannot know thy change,
In many's looks, the false heart's history
Is writ in moods and frowns and wrinkles strange:
But heaven in thy creation did decree
That in thy face sweet love should ever dwell,
Whate'er thy thoughts, or thy heart's workings be,
Thy looks should nothing thence but sweetness tell.
How like Eve's apple doth thy beauty grow,
If thy sweet virtue answer not thy show.

Q140

Be wise as thou art cruel, do not press
My tongue-tied patience with too much disdain:
Lest sorrow lend me words and words express
The manner of my pity-wanting pain.
If I might teach thee wit, better it were
Though not to love, yet (love) to tell me so,
As testy sick-men when their deaths be near
No news but health from their Physicians know.
For if I should despair I should grow mad,
And in my madness might speak ill of thee,
Now this ill-wresting world is grown so bad,
Mad slanderers by mad ears believed be.
That I may not be so, nor thou belied,
Bear thine eyes straight, though thy proud heart go wide.

See longer notes for relocation and reversal of this leaf.

Q139

O call not me to justify the wrong
That thy unkindness lays upon my heart,
Wound me not with thine eye but with thy tongue,
Use power with power, and slay me not by Art,
Tell me thou lov'st elsewhere; but in my sight
Dear heart forbear to glance thine eye aside,
What needst thou wound with cunning when thy might
Is more than my o'erpress'd defence can bide?
Let me excuse thee, "ah my love well knows
Her pretty looks have been mine enemies,
And therefore from my face she turns my foes,
That they elsewhere might dart their injuries:"
Yet do not so, but since I am near slain,
Kill me outright with looks, and rid my pain.

Q94

They that have power to hurt, and will do none,
That do not do the thing they most do show,
Who moving others, are themselves as stone,
Unmoved, cold, and to temptation slow:
They rightly do inherit heaven's graces,
And husband nature's riches from expense,
They are the Lords and owners of their faces,
Others, but stewards of their excellence:
The summer's flower is to the summer sweet,
Though to itself, it only live and die,
But if that flower with base infection meet,
The basest weed out-braves his dignity:
For sweetest things turn sourest by their deeds,
Lilies that fester smell far worse than weeds.

Real sun-kings have power to kill with looks but do not
abuse it. Those who are only flowers need the faithfulness
of the Girasol to avoid canker.

Q95

How sweet and lovely dost thou make the shame
Which like a canker in the fragrant Rose
Doth spot the beauty of thy budding name?
Oh in what sweets dost thou thy sins enclose!
That tongue that tells the story of thy days
(Making lascivious comments on thy sport)
Cannot dispraise, but in a kind of praise,
Naming thy name, blesses an ill report.
Oh what a mansion have those vices got
Which for their habitation chose out thee,
Where beauty's veil doth cover every blot,
And all things turns to fair, that eyes can see!
Take heed (dear heart) of this large privilege,
The hardest knife ill us'd doth lose his edge.

Q96

Some say thy fault is youth, some wantonness,
Some say thy grace is youth and gentle sport,
Both grace and faults are lov'd of more and less:
Thou mak'st faults graces, that to thee resort:
As on the finger of a throned Queen
The basest Jewel will be well esteem'd:
So are those errors that in thee are seen
To truths translated, and for true things deem'd.
How many Lambs might the stern Wolf betray
If like a Lamb he could his looks translate.
How many gazers mightst thou lead away
If thou wouldst use the strength of all thy state?
† But do not so, I love thee in such sort
As thou being mine, mine is thy good report.

The couplet is † borrowed from Q36 which is unprecedented.
The freelance scholar Stephen Barber suggests that what
was censored from here was Orsino's couplet *Twelfth Night*
5.ii.124-5 also in a context of mistaken identity and gender,

I'll sacrifice the lamb that I do love
To spite a raven's heart within a dove

See longer notes.

Q97

How like a Winter hath my absence been
From thee, the pleasure of the fleeting year?
What freezings have I felt, what dark days seen?
What old December's bareness every where?
And yet this time remov'd was summer's time,
And teeming Autumn big with rich increase,
Bearing the wanton burthen of the prime
Like widow'd wombs after their Lords' decease:
Yet this abundant issue seem'd to me
But hope of Orphans, and unfather'd fruit,
For Summer and his pleasures wait on thee,
And thou away, the very birds are mute.
Or if they sing, tis with so dull a cheer
That leaves look pale, dreading the Winter's near.

This and the next two seem to deputise for the account of his
absence after it was cut out of this place in the Notebook.

Q98

From you have I been absent in the spring,
When proud pied April (dress'd in all his trim)
Hath put a spirit of youth in every thing:
That heavy Saturn laugh'd and leap'd with him.
Yet nor the lays of birds, nor the sweet smell
Of different flowers in odour and in hue
Could make me any summer's story tell:
Or from their proud lap pluck them where they grew:
Nor did I wonder at the Lily's white,
Nor praise the deep vermilion in the Rose,
They were but sweet, but figures of delight:
Drawn after you, you pattern of all those.
Yet seem'd it Winter still, and you away,
As with your shadow I with these did play.

Q99

The forward violet thus did I chide,
Sweet thief whence didst thou steal thy sweet that smells
If not from my love's breath, the purple pride,
Which on thy soft cheek for complexion dwells?
In my love's veins thou has too grossly dyed,
The Lily I condemned for thy hand,
And buds of marjoram had stol'n thy hair,
The Roses fearfully on thorns did stand,
One blushing shame, an other white despair:
A third, nor red nor white, had stol'n of both,
And to his robbery had annex'd thy breath,
But for his theft in pride of all his growth
A vengeful canker ate him up to death.
More flowers I noted, yet I none could see
But sweet or colour it had stol'n from thee. .

Without the anomalous fifteenth line, this could be
addressed to the "sweet thief" of Q35.14.

Q113

Since I left you, mine eye is in my mind,
And that which governs me to go about
Doth part his function, and is partly blind,
Seems seeing, but effectually is out:
For it no form delivers to the heart
Of bird, of flower, or shape which it doth latch,
Of his quick objects hath the mind no part,
Nor his own vision holds what it doth catch:
For if it see the rud'st or gentlest sight,
The most sweet-favour or deformedst creature,
The mountain or the sea, the day or night,
The Crow or Dove, it shapes them to your feature.
Incapable of more, replete with you,
My most true mind thus maketh mine untrue.

Obviously out of place in Q where it comes in the group
about return to the friend. It should begin the self-exile.
See longer notes.
Line 12 links with the animal imagery of Q96.
Dove = a true lover, a crow is the opposite.
See longer notes on this and the next five sonnets.

Q114

Or whether doth my mind being crown'd with you
Drink up the monarch's plague this flattery?
Or whether shall I say mine eye saith true,
And that your love taught it this Alchemy?
To make of monsters, and things indigest,
Such cherubins as your sweet self resemble,
Creating every bad a perfect best
As fast as objects to his beams assemble:
Oh tis the first, tis flattery in my seeing,
And my great mind most kingly drinks it up,
Mine eye well knows what with his gust is 'greeing,
And to his palate doth prepare the cup.
If it be poison'd, tis the lesser sin
That mine eye loves it and doth first begin.

Line 1 "crown'd with you" since the friend is not present
must mean the state of being "in sleep a king" (Q87.14).
A love potion will cause Cupid's kind of blindness.
The emphatic "begin" demands a sequel from a dramatist,
cf. Q35.11 "commence". See longer notes.

Q148

O me! What eyes hath love put in my head,
Which have no correspondence with true sight,
Or if they have, where is my judgment fled,
That censures falsely what they see aright?
If that be fair whereon my false eyes dote,
What means the world to say it is not so?
If it be not, then love doth well denote,
Love's eye is not so true as all men's: no,
How can it? O how can love's eye be true,
That is so vex'd with watching and with tears?
No marvel then though I mistake my view,
The sun itself sees not, till heaven clears.
O cunning love, with tears thou keepst me blind,
Lest eyes well seeing thy foul faults should find.

The alternatives of the first quatrain are the same as
those of Q114. This must be transitional between an
old love and a new, see p. xix - xx and longer notes.
Line 7 it is tempting to read 'lore' instead of 'love'.

Q147

My love is as a fever longing still
For that which longer nurseth the disease,
Feeding on that which doth preserve the ill,
The uncertain sickly appetite to please:
My reason the Physician to my love
Angry that his prescriptions are not kept
Hath left me, and I desperate now approve
Desire is death, which Physic did except.
Past cure I am, now Reason is past care,
And frantic mad with evermore unrest,
My thoughts and my discourse as mad men's are,
At random from the truth vainly express'd.
For I have sworn thee fair, and thought thee bright,
Who art as black as hell, as dark as night.

See longer notes.

Q129

The expense of Spirit in a waste of shame
Is lust in action, and till action, lust
Is perjur'd, murderous, bloody full of blame,
Savage, extreme, rude, cruel, not to trust,
Enjoy'd no sooner but despised straight,
Past reason hunted, and no sooner had
Past reason hated, as a swallowed bait
On purpose laid to make the taker mad:
Mad in pursuit and in possession so,
Had, having, and in quest to have extreme,
A bliss in proof and prov'd a very woe,
Before a joy proposed, behind a dream;
All this the world well knows yet none knows well
To shun the heaven that leads men to this hell.

A philosophic rather than a moral critique of lust –
what does not last is not real. It changes its nature to the
opposite five times within a single line of verse.

Q130

My Mistress' eyes are nothing like the Sun,
Coral is far more red than her lips' red,
If snow be white, why then her breasts are dun;
If hairs be wires, black wires grow on her head;
I have seen Roses damask'd, red and white,
But no such Roses see I in her cheeks,
And in some perfumes is there more delight
Than in the breath that from my Mistress reeks.
I love to hear her speak, yet well I know
That Music hath a far more pleasing sound;
I grant I never saw a goddess go,
My Mistress when she walks treads on the ground.
And yet by heaven I think my love as rare
As any she belied with false compare.

The depressive phase of Q129's manic depressive cycle.
See longer notes.

Q131

Thou art as tyrannous, so as thou art,
As those whose beauties proudly make them cruel;
For well thou know'st to my dear doting heart
Thou art the fairest and most precious Jewel.
Yet in good faith some say that thee behold
Thy face hath not the power to make love groan;
To say they err, I dare not be so bold,
Although I swear it to my self alone.
And to be sure that is not false I swear,
A thousand groans but thinking on thy face
One on another's neck do witness bear
Thy black is fairest in my judgment's place.
In nothing art thou black save in thy deeds,
And thence this slander as I think proceeds.

Line 13 gives the lady's darkness only a metaphorical
meaning; See p. xix.

Q132

Thine eyes I love, and they as pitying me,
Knowing thy heart torments me with disdain,
Have put on black, and loving mourners be,
Looking with pretty ruth upon my pain.
And truly not the morning Sun of Heaven
Better becomes the grey cheeks of the East,
Nor that full Star that ushers in the Even
Doth half that glory to the sober West
As those two mourning eyes become thy face:
O let it then as well beseem thy heart
To mourn for me, since mourning doth thee grace,
And suit thy pity like in every part.
Then will I swear Beauty her self is black,
And all they foul that thy complexion lack.

Q127

In the old age black was not counted fair,
Or if it were it bore not beauty's name:
But now is black beauty's successive heir,
And Beauty slander'd with a bastard shame,
For since each hand hath put on Nature's power,
Fairing the foul with Art's false borrow'd face,
Sweet Beauty hath no name, no holy bower,
But is profan'd, if not lives in disgrace.
Therefore my Mistress' hairs are Raven black,
Her eyes so suited, and they mourners seem
At such who not born fair no beauty lack,
Slandering Creation with a false esteem;
Yet so they mourn, becoming of their woe,
That every tongue says Beauty should look so.

Passionate
Pilgrim No. 3

Did not the heavenly rhetoric of thine eye,
Gainst whom the world could not hold argument,
Persuade my heart to this false perjury?
Vows for thee broke deserve not punishment.
A woman I forswore: but I will prove
Thou being a Goddess, I forswore not thee:
My vow was earthly, thou a heavenly love,
Thy grace being gain'd cures all disgrace in me.
My vow was breath, and breath a vapour is.
Then thou fair Sun, that on this earth doth shine,
Exhale this vapour vow, in thee it is:
If broken, then it is no fault of mine.
If by me broke, what fool is not so wise
To break an oath to win a Paradise?

Of the first three sonnets in The *Passionate Pilgrim*,
No. 1 is virtually the same as Q138 here and No.2 is
Q144. No.3 occurs in the text of *Love's Labours Lost*,
and is imported here as a much likelier partner to Q138
than Q128 for which see Supplement (it has no concerns
in common with the other sonnets, this has many).

Q138
(*Passionate
Pilgrim* No. 1)

When my love swears that she is made of truth,
I do believe her though I know she lies,
That she might think me some untutor'd youth,
Unlearned in the world's false subtleties.
Thus vainly thinking that she thinks me young,
Although she knows my days are past the best,
Simply I credit her false speaking tongue,
On both sides thus is simple truth suppress'd:
But wherefore says she not she is unjust?
And wherefore say not I that I am old?
O love's best habit is in seeming trust,
And age in love, loves not t' have years told.
Therefore I lie with her, and she with me,
And in our faults by lies we flattered be.

One of the few (surely?) which reads as if it could be
addressed to a real woman; tender-minded, it longs for
a moment of truth.

Q137

Thou blind fool love, what dost thou to mine eyes,
That they behold and see not what they see:
They know what beauty is, see where it lies,
Yet what the best is, take the worst to be.
If eyes corrupt by over-partial looks
Be anchor'd in the bay where all men ride,
Why of eyes' falsehood hast thou forged hooks
Whereto the judgment of my heart is tied?
Why should my heart think that a several plot
Which my heart knows the wide world's common place?
Or mine eyes seeing this, say this is not,
To put fair truth upon so foul a face?
In things right true my heart and eyes have erred,
And to this false plague are they now transferred.

The harsh tone reflects the Platonist emphasis on falsehood,
the witchcraft-generated phantom is delusory not just unfaithful.
Prepares for reintroducing the friend as fellow victim.
Line 14 "transferred": the term used also by modern
psychoanalysis. The plan of these sonnets seems to be that
she is 1) dark 2) false 3) cruel. See note on Q105.

Q141

In faith I do not love thee with mine eyes,
For they in thee a thousand errors note,
But tis my heart that loves what they despise,
Who in despite of view is pleas'd to dote:
Nor are mine ears with thy tongue's tune delighted,
Nor tender feeling to base touches prone,
Nor taste, nor smell, desire to be invited
To any sensual feast with thee alone:
But my five wits nor my five senses can
Dissuade one foolish heart from serving thee,
Who leaves unsway'd the likeness of a man,
Thy proud heart's slave and vassal wretch to be:
Only my plague thus far I count my gain,
That she that makes me sin, awards me pain.

She is repulsive to all five senses, the Loathly Lady;
so how can 'heart' come into it? Could possibly mean
"my friend", since the notion that they have exchanged
hearts seemed very literal in earlier sonnets.

Q142

Love is my sin, and thy dear virtue hate,
Hate of my sin, grounded on sinful loving;
O but with mine, compare thou thine own state,
And thou shalt find it merits not reproving,
Or if it do, not from those lips of thine
That have profan'd their scarlet ornaments
And seal'd false bonds of love as oft as mine,
Robb'd others' beds' revenues of their rents.
Be it lawful I love thee as thou lov'st those
Whom thine eyes woo as mine importune thee,
Root pity in thy heart that when it grows
Thy pity may deserve to pitied be.
If thou dost seek to have what thou dost hide,
By self-example mayst thou be denied.

Q135

Who ever hath her wish, thou hast thy *Will*,
And *Will* to boot, and *Will* in over-plus,
More than enough am I that vex thee still,
To thy sweet will making addition thus.
Wilt thou whose will is large and spacious
Not once vouchsafe to hide my will in thine,
Shall will in others seem right gracious,
And in my will no fair acceptance shine?
The sea all water, yet receives rain still,
And in abundance addeth to his store,
So thou being rich in *Will* add to thy *Will*
One will of mine to make thy large *Will* more.
Let 'No' unkind, no fair beseechers kill.
Think all but one, and me in that one *Will*.

Q136

If thy soul check thee that I come so near,
Swear to thy blind soul that I was thy *Will*,
And will thy soul knows is admitted there,
Thus far for love my love-suit sweet fulfil.
Will will fulfil the treasure of thy love,
Ay fills it full with wills, and my will one;
In things of great receipt with ease we prove
Among a number one is reckon'd none:
Then in the number let me pass untold,
Though in thy store's account I one must be,
For nothing hold me, so it please thee hold
That nothing me, a something sweet to thee.
Make but my name thy love, and love that still,
And then thou lovest me for my name's *Will*.

These phallic sonnets give his case against promiscuity in its
extreme form - she does not know one owner of will (name
or organ) from another. The plan of these Sonnets seems to be
that she is 1) dark, 2) false, 3) cruel.
See note on Q105.

Q143

Lo as a careful housewife runs to catch
One of her feathered creatures broke away,
Sets down her babe and makes all swift despatch
In pursuit of the thing she would have stay:
Whilst her neglected child holds her in chase,
Cries to catch her whose busy care is bent
To follow that which flies before her face:
Not prizing her poor infant's discontent;
So runn'st thou after that which flies from thee,
Whilst I thy babe chase thee afar behind,
But if thou catch thy hope turn back to me:
And play the mother's part, kiss me, be kind.
So will I pray that thou mayst have thy *Will*,
If thou turn back and my loud crying still.

The tragic triangle becomes a comedy, acted by a hen-wife,
hen and toddler. That the phantom can turn into a hen
reminds of the kind of magic that happens in Marlowe's *Faust*.

Q144
(*Passionate Pilgrim* No 2)

Two loves I have of comfort and despair,
Which like two spirits do suggest me still,
The better angel is a man right fair:
The worser spirit a woman colour'd ill.
To win me soon to hell my female evil
Tempteth my better angel from my side,
And would corrupt my saint to be a devil:
Wooing his purity with her foul pride.
And whether that my angel be turn'd fiend
Suspect I may, yet not directly tell,
But being both from me, both to each friend,
I guess one angel in an other's hell.
Yet this shall I ne'er know but live in doubt,
Till my bad angel fire my good one out.

A grimmer diagnosis of the triangle - what if my two loves
are just one, my angel has turned fiend? For syphilis as
metaphor in the last line cf. Q147 and Qs. 153-4.
Lines 9-10 bear out this edition's thesis of mistaken identity
as the plot of Series II

Q133

Beshrew that heart that makes my heart to groan
For that deep wound it gives my friend and me;
Is't not enough to torture me alone,
But slave to slavery my sweet'st friend must be.
Me from my self thy cruel eye hath taken
And my next self thou harder hast engrossed,
Of him, my self, and thee I am forsaken,
A torment thrice threefold thus to be crossed:
Prison my heart in thy steel bosom's ward,
But then my friend's heart let my poor heart bail,
Whoe'er keeps me, let my heart be his guard,
Thou canst not then use rigour in my jail.
And yet thou wilt, for I being pent in thee
Perforce am thine and all that is in me.

She is cruel to both men so sympathy with his friend
becomes possible again.

Q134

So now I have confess'd that he is thine,
And I my self am mortgag'd to thy will;
My self I'll forfeit, so that other mine
Thou wilt restore to be my comfort still:
But thou wilt not, nor he will not be free,
For thou art covetous, and he is kind,
He learn'd but surety-like to write for me
Under that bond that him as fast doth bind.
The statute of thy beauty thou wilt take,
Thou usurer that putt'st forth all to use,
And sue a friend came debter for my sake,
So him I lose through my unkind abuse.
Him have I lost, thou hast both him and me,
He pays the whole, and yet am I not free.

To see the friend as fellow victim prepares the way for
reconciliation.

Q149

Canst thou, O cruel, say I love thee not,
When I against my self with thee partake:
Do I not think on thee when I forgot
Am of my self, all tyrant for thy sake?
Who hateth thee that I do call my friend,
On whom frown'st thou that I do fawn upon,
Nay if thou lour'st on me do I not spend
Revenge upon my self with present moan?
What merit do I in my self respect
That is so proud thy service to despise,
When all my best doth worship thy defect,
Commanded by the motion of thine eyes.
But love hate on for now I know thy mind,
Those that can see thou lov'st, and I am blind.

For Q149 ff. See longer notes.

Q150

Oh from what power hast thou this powerful might,
With insufficiency my heart to sway,
To make me give the lie to my true sight
And swear that brightness doth not grace the day?
Whence hast thou this becoming of things ill,
That in the very refuse of thy deeds
There is such strength and warrantise of skill
That in my mind thy worst all best exceeds?
Who taught thee how to make me love thee more
The more I hear and see just cause of hate?
Oh though I love what others do abhor,
With others thou shouldst not abhor my state.
If thy unworthiness rais'd love in me,
More worthy I to be belov'd of thee.

Q151

Love is too young to know what conscience is,
Yet who knows not conscience is born of love;
Then gentle cheater urge not my amiss,
Lest guilty of my faults thy sweet self prove.
For thou betraying me, I do betray
My nobler part to my gross body's treason,
My soul doth tell my body that he may
Triumph in love, flesh stays no farther reason,
But rising at thy name doth point out thee
As his triumphant prize, proud of this pride
He is contented thy poor drudge to be
To stand in thy affairs, fall by thy side.
No want of conscience hold it that I call
Her love, for whose dear love I rise and fall.

See longer notes.

Q152

In loving thee thou know'st I am forsworn,
But thou art twice forsworn to me love swearing,
In act thy bed-vow broke and new faith torn,
In vowing new hate after new love bearing:
But why of two oaths' breach do I accuse thee,
When I break twenty: I am perjur'd most,
For all my vows are oaths but to misuse thee:
And all my honest faith in thee is lost.
For I have sworn deep oaths of thy deep kindness:
Oaths of thy love, thy truth, thy constancy,
And to enlighten thee gave eyes to blindness
Or made them swear against the thing they see.
For I have sworn thee fair: more perjur'd eye,
To swear against the truth so foul a lie.

See longer notes.
Lines 13-14 As a climatic self-accusation "I have called
you better-looking than you are" is sheer bathos.
Unless it means "I have taken you for someone else who
was fair".

Q146

Poor soul the centre of my sinful earth,
My sins these rebel powers that thee array,
Why dost thou pine within and suffer dearth
Painting thy outward walls so costly gay?
Why so large cost having so short a lease
Dost thou upon thy fading mansion spend?
Shall worms inheritors of this excess
Eat up thy charge? is this thy body's end?
Then soul live thou upon thy servant's loss,
And let that pine to aggravate thy store;
Buy terms divine in selling hours of dross:
Within be fed, without be rich no more,
So shalt thou feed on death, that feeds on men,
And death once dead, there's no more dying then.
Line 2 *'My sins these read'* by Bulloch.
Q 'My sinful earth these'.

A fine sonnet but does not seem to belong, unless as regret for his sins - cf. *Lucrece* ll. 714, 722, sexual desire as "the guilty rebel".

Q145

Those lips that Love's own hand did make
Breath'd forth the sound that said I hate
To me that languish'd for her sake:
But when she saw my woeful state,
Straight in her heart did mercy come,
Chiding that tongue that ever sweet
Was us'd in giving gentle doom:
And taught it thus anew to greet:
I hate she alter'd with an end
That follow'd it as gentle day
Doth follow night who like a fiend
From heaven to hell is flown away.
I hate, from hate away she threw
And sav'd my life saying Not you.

Line 13 puns on Anne Hathaway's name.
See longer notes.

Q153

Cupid laid by his brand and fell asleep,
A maid of Dian's this advantage found,
And his love-kindling fire did quickly steep
In a cold valley-fountain of that ground:
Which borrow'd from this holy fire of love
A dateless lively heat still to endure,
And grew a seething bath which yet men prove
Against strange maladies a sovereign cure:
But at my mistress' eye love's brand new fired,
The boy for trial needs would touch my breast,
I sick withal the help of bath desired,
And thither hied a sad distemper'd guest.
But found no cure, the bath for my help lies
Where Cupid got new fire; my mistress' eye.

This and the next relate to the "tub" cure for syphilis, and
their purpose must be to merit Q100's contempt for the
recent material, "some worthless song".

Q154

The little Love-God lying once asleep
Laid by his side his heart-enflaming brand,
Whilst many Nymphs that vow'd chaste life to keep
Came tripping by, but in her maiden hand
The fairest votary took up that fire,
Which many legions of true hearts had warm'd,
And so the General of hot desire
Was sleeping by a Virgin hand disarm'd.
This brand she quenched in a cool Well by,
Which from love's fire took heat perpetual,
Growing a bath and healthful remedy
For men diseas'd; but I my Mistress' thrall
Came there for cure and this by that I prove,
Love's fire heats water, water cools not love.

Q100

Where art thou Muse that thou forget'st so long
To speak of that which gives thee all thy might?
Spend'st thou thy fury on some worthless song,
Darkening thy power to lend base subjects light.
Return forgetful Muse, and straight redeem
In gentle numbers time so idly spent,
Sing to the ear that doth thy lays esteem
And gives thy pen both skill and argument.
Rise resty Muse, my love's sweet face survey,
If time have any wrinkle graven there,
If any, be a Satire to decay,
And make time's spoils despised everywhere.
Give my love fame faster than time wastes life,
So thou prevent'st his scythe and crooked knife.

The poet is too serious-minded to have read the "dark"
and "base" material his Muse has been busy with.

Q101

Oh truant Muse, what shall be thy amends
For thy neglect of truth in beauty dyed?
Both truth and beauty on my love depends:
So dost thou too, and therein dignified;
Make answer Muse, wilt thou not haply say
Truth needs no colour with his colour fix'd,
Beauty no pencil, beauty's truth to lay:
But best is best, if never intermix'd.
Because he needs no praise, wilt thou be dumb?
Excuse not silence so, for 't lies in thee
To make him much outlive a gilded tomb,
And to be prais'd of ages yet to be.
Then do thy office, Muse, I teach thee how
To make him seem long hence as he shows now.

"I teach thee how" demotes the Muse!

Q102

My love is strengthen'd though more weak in seeming,
I love not less, though less the show appear;
That love is merchandis'd whose rich esteeming
The owner's tongue doth publish everywhere.
Our love was new, and then but in the spring,
When I was wont to greet it with my lays,
As Philomel in summer's front doth sing,
And stops his pipe in growth of riper days:
Not that the summer is less pleasant now
Than when her mournful hymns did hush the night,
But that wild music burthens every bough,
And sweets grown common lose their dear delight.
Therefore like her, I sometime hold my tongue:
Because I would not dull you with my song.

Philomel is bisexual, first 'his' then 'her'.
Reverts to the theme of too many rival poets.

Q103

Alack what poverty my Muse brings forth,
That having such a scope to show her pride,
The argument all bare is of more worth
Than when it hath my added praise beside.
Oh blame me not if I no more can write!
Look in your glass and there appears a face
That overgoes my blunt invention quite,
Dulling my lines, and doing me disgrace.
Were it not sinful then, striving to mend,
To mar the subject that before was well?
For to no other pass my verses tend
Than of your graces and your gifts to tell.
And more, much more than in my verse can sit
Your own glass shows you when you look in it.

Nature is better than art.
He is excusing his silence, which was complained of in Q83.

Q104

To me fair friend you never can be old,
For as you were when first your eye I eyed
Such seems your beauty still. Three Winters cold
Have from the forests shook three summers' pride,
Three beauteous springs to yellow Autumn turned,
In process of the seasons have I seen,
Three April perfumes in three hot Junes burn'd,
Since first I saw you fresh which yet are green.
Ah yet doth beauty like a dial hand
Steal from his figure, and no pace perceived,
So your sweet hue, which methinks still doth stand,
Hath motion, and mine eye may be deceived.
For fear of which, hear this thou age unbred,
Ere you were born was beauty's summer dead.

Line 7f. Presumably the years '92-94

135

Q105

Let not my love be call'd Idolatry,
Nor my beloved as an Idol show,
Since all alike my songs and praises be
To one, of one, still such, and ever so.
Kind is my love today, tomorrow kind,
Still constant in a wondrous excellence,
Therefore my verse to constancy confin'd,
One thing expressing, leaves out difference.
Fair, kind and true, is all my argument,
Fair, kind and true, varying to other words,
And in this change is my invention spent,
Three themes in one, which wondrous scope affords.
Fair, kind, and true have often liv'd alone:
Which three till now, never kept seat in one.

Line 10 In the mistress episode he varied the words to
dark, false and cruel.

136

Q106

When in the chronicle of wasted time
I see descriptions of the fairest wights,
And beauty making beautiful old rhyme,
In praise of Ladies dead, and lovely Knights,
Then in the blazon of sweet beauty's best,
Of hand, of foot, of lip, of eye, of brow,
I see their antique pen would have express'd
Even such a beauty as you master now.
So all their praises are but prophecies
Of this our time, all you prefiguring,
And for they look'd but with divining eyes
They had not skill enough your worth to sing:
For we which now behold these present days
Have eyes to wonder, but lack tongues to praise.

This and the next take up "idolatry" from Q105.
The World Soul needs the phoenix ideal.
cf. the superb sextet of Q108.

Q107

Not mine own fears, nor the prophetic soul
Of the wide world, dreaming on things to come,
Can yet the lease of my true love control,
Suppos'd as forfeit to a confin'd doom.
The mortal Moon hath her eclipse endur'd,
And the sad Augurs mock their own presage,
Incertainties now crown themselves assur'd,
And peace proclaims olives of endless age.
Now with the drops of this most balmy time
My love looks fresh, and death to me subscribes,
Since spite of him I'll live in this poor rhyme,
While he insults o'er dull and speechless tribes.
And thou in this shalt find thy monument,
When tyrants' crests and tombs of brass are spent.

See longer notes. Line 12 'he' = death.

Q108

What's in the brain that ink may character
Which hath not figur'd to thee my true spirit,
What's new to speak, what now to register,
That may express my love or thy dear merit?
Nothing sweet boy, but yet like prayers divine
I must each day say o'er the very same,
Counting no old thing old, thou mine, I thine,
Even as when first I hallowed thy fair name.
So that eternal love in love's fresh case
Weighs not the dust and injury of age,
Nor gives to necessary wrinkles place,
But makes antiquity for aye his page,
Finding the first conceit of love there bred
Where time and outward form would show it dead.

What more is there to say? Is a *coup de théâtre* to provoke
the friend's protest; he has read the mistress sonnets even
if the poet claims in Q100 that he himself hasn't.

Q109

O never say that I was false of heart,
Though absence seem'd my flame to qualify,
As easy might I from my self depart
As from my soul which in thy breast doth lie:
That is my home of love, if I have rang'd
Like him that travels I return again,
Just to the time, not with the time exchang'd,
So that my self bring water for my stain;
Never believe, though in my nature reign'd
All frailties that besiege all kinds of blood,
That it could so preposterously be stain'd
To leave for nothing all thy sum of good:
For nothing this wide Universe I call
Save thou my Rose, in it thou art my all.

I have been acting a part - worse essays in love were
to prove you my best one; "newer proof". Q110 line 11
assumes the friend will take the mistress episode
realistically not allegorically.

Q110

Alas tis true, I have gone here and there,
And made my self a motley to the view,
Gor'd mine own thoughts, sold cheap what is most dear,
Made old offences of affections new.
Most true it is, that I have look'd on truth
Askance and strangely: but by all above,
These blenches gave my heart an other youth,
And worse essays prov'd thee my best of love.
Now all is done, have what shall have no end,
Mine appetite I never more will grind
On newer proof, to try an older friend,
A God in love, to whom I am confin'd.
Then give me welcome, next my heaven the best,
Even to thy pure and most most loving breast.

Q111

O for my sake do you with fortune chide,
The guilty goddess of my harmful deeds,
That did not better for my life provide
Than public means which public manners breeds.
Thence comes it that my name receives a brand,
And almost thence my nature is subdu'd
To what it works in, like the Dyer's hand;
Pity me then, and wish I were renew'd,
Whilst like a willing patient I will drink
Potions of eisel gainst my strong infection,
No bitterness that I will bitter think,
Nor double penance to correct correction.
Pity me then dear friend, and I assure ye,
Even that your pity is enough to cure me.

He does not wish to go back to the stage.

Q112

Your love and pity doth the impression fill
Which vulgar scandal stamp'd upon my brow,
For what care I who calls me well or ill,
So you o'er-green my bad, my good allow?
You are my All the world and I must strive
To know my shames and praises from your tongue,
None else to me, nor I to none alive,
That my steel'd sense or changes right or wrong.
In so profound abysm I throw all care
Of others' voices, that my Adder's sense
To critic and to flatterer stopped are:
Mark how with my neglect I do dispense,
You are so strongly in my purpose bred,
That all the world besides me thinks y' are dead.

Line 14 *Avisa* asserted that its fictional Henry Willoby
had died.

143

Q115

Those lines that I before have writ do lie,
Even those that said I could not love you dearer,
Yet then my judgment knew no reason why
My most full flame should afterwards burn clearer.
But reckoning time, whose million'd accidents
Creep in twixt vows, and change decrees of Kings,
Tan sacred beauty, blunt the sharp'st intents,
Divert strong minds to th' course of altering things:
Alas why fearing of time's tyranny
Might I not then say, now I love you best,
When I was certain o'er incertainty,
Crowning the present, doubting of the rest:
Love is a Babe, then might I not say so
To give full growth to that which still doth grow.

Q115.1 the orator's device of offering a weakness then
proving it a strength.

Q116

Let me not to the marriage of true minds
Admit impediments, love is not love
Which alters when it alteration finds,
Or bends with the remover to remove.
O no, it is an ever fixed mark
That looks on tempests and is never shaken;
It is the star to every wandering bark,
Whose worth's unknown, although his height be taken.
Love's not Time's fool, though rosy lips and cheeks
Within his bending sickle's compass come,
Love alters not with his brief hours and weeks,
But bears it out even to the edge of doom:
If this be error and upon me proved,
I never writ, nor no man ever loved.

Not a defeatist ending. We know that he did write,
so the If clause cannot hold good.

Q117

Accuse me thus, that I have scanted all
Wherein I should your great deserts repay,
Forgot upon your dearest love to call,
Whereto all bonds do tie me day by day,
That I have frequent been with unknown minds
And given to time your own dear purchas'd right,
That I have hoisted sail to all the winds
Which should transport me farthest from your sight.
Book both my wilfulness and errors down,
And on just proof surmise accumulate,
Bring me within the level of your frown,
But shoot not at me in your waken'd hate:
Since my appeal says I did strive to prove
The constancy and virtue of your love.

See longer notes on Qs 117-9.

Q118

Like as to make our appetites more keen
With eager compounds we our palate urge,
As to prevent our maladies unseen
We sicken to shun sickness when we purge,
Even so being full of your ne'er cloying sweetness
To bitter sauces did I frame my feeding;
And sick of welfare found a kind of meetness
To be diseas'd ere that there was true needing.
Thus policy in love to anticipate
The ills that were not, grew to faults assured,
And brought to medicine a healthful state
Which rank of goodness would by ill be cured.
But thence I learn and find the lesson true,
Drugs poison him that so fell sick of you.

Q119

What potions have I drunk of Siren tears
Distill'd from limbecks foul as hell within,
Applying fears to hopes and hopes to fears,
Still losing when I saw my self to win?
What wretched errors hath my heart committed
Whilst it hath thought itself so blessed never?
How have mine eyes out of their spheres been fitted
In the distraction of this madding fever?
O benefit of ill, now I find true
That better is by evil still made better,
And ruin'd love when it is built anew
Grows fairer than at first, more strong, far greater.
So I return rebuk'd to my content,
And gain by ills thrice more than I have spent.

Q120

That you were once unkind befriends me now,
And for that sorrow, which I then did feel,
Needs must I under my transgression bow,
Unless my nerves were brass or hammered steel.
For if you were by my unkindness shaken
As I by yours, you have passed a hell of Time,
And I a tyrant have no leisure taken
To weigh how once I suffered in your crime.
O that our night of woe might have remember'd
My deepest sense, how hard true sorrow hits,
And soon to you, as you to me then, tender'd
The humble salve which wounded bosoms fits!
But that your trespass now becomes a fee,
Mine ransoms yours, and yours must ransom me.

Line 7 tyrant = not governed by the principles of justice.
Line 9 refers back to Q34.

Q121

Tis better to be vile than vile esteemed,
When not to be, receives reproach of being,
And the just pleasure lost, which is so deemed
Not by our feeling, but by others' seeing.
For why should others' false adulterate eyes
Give salutation to my sportive blood?
Or on my frailties why are frailer spies,
Which in their wills count bad what I think good?
No, I am that I am, and they that level
At my abuses, reckon up their own,
I may be straight though they themselves be bevel:
By their rank thoughts, my deeds must not be shown
Unless this general evil they maintain,
All men are bad and in their badness reign.

See p. xvii.

Q123

No! Time, thou shalt not boast that I do change,
Thy pyramids built up with newer might
To me are nothing novel, nothing strange,
They are but dressings of a former sight:
Our dates are brief, and therefore we admire
What thou dost foist upon us that is old,
And rather make them born to our desire
Than think that we before have heard them told:
Thy registers and thee I both defy,
Not wondering at the present, nor the past,
For thy records and what we see doth lie,
Made more or less by thy continual haste;
This I do vow and this shall ever be,
I will be true despite thy scythe and thee.

Q124

If my dear love were but the child of state,
It might for fortune's bastard be unfather'd,
As subject to time's love, or to time's hate,
Weeds among weeds, or flowers with flowers gather'd.
No it was builded far from accident,
It suffers not in smiling pomp, nor falls
Under the blow of thralled discontent
Whereto the inviting time our fashion calls:
It fears not policy that Heretic,
Which works on leases of short numbered hours,
But all alone stands hugely politic,
That it nor grows with heat, nor drowns with showers.
To this I witness call the fools of time,
Which die for goodness, who have liv'd for crime.

See longer notes and p. 177.

Q125

Were 't aught to me I bore the canopy,
With my extern the outward honouring,
Or laid great bases for eternity
Which proves more short than waste or ruining?
Have I not seen dwellers on form and favour
Lose all and more by paying too much rent
For compound sweet; forgoing simple savour,
Pitiful thrivers in their gazing spent.
No, let me be obsequious in thy heart,
And take thou my oblation, poor but free,
Which is not mix'd with seconds, knows no art
But mutual render, only me for thee.
Hence, thou suborn'd Informer, a true soul
When most impeach'd, stands least in thy control.

Could perhaps relate to some ceremony for H.W.'s
21st birthday? which was on 6th October 1594.
Line 13 cf. "spies" Q121.7 and p. xix.

Q126

O thou my lovely Boy who in thy hour
Dost hold time's fickle glass, his sickle power:
Who hast by waning grown, and therein show'st
Thy lovers withering, as thy sweet self grow'st,
If Nature (sovereign mistress over wrack)
As thou goest onwards still will pluck thee back,
She keeps thee to this purpose, that her skill
May time disgrace, and wretched minutes kill.
Yet fear her O thou minion of her pleasure,
She may detain, but not still keep her treasure!
Her audit though delay'd answer'd must be,
And her quietus is to render thee.
Q Line 1 power   line 2 hour

See longer notes.

Envoi

Q122

Thy gift, thy tables, are within my brain
Full character'd with lasting memory,
Which shall above that idle rank remain
Beyond all date even to eternity.
Or at the least, so long as brain and heart
Have faculty by nature to subsist,
Till each to raz'd oblivion yield his part
Of thee, thy record never can be miss'd:
That poor retention could not so much hold,
Nor need I tallies thy dear love to score,
Therefore to give them from me was I bold,
To trust those tables that receive thee more;
To keep an adjunct to remember thee
Were to import forgetfulness in me.

The second Notebook sonnet.
As the last poem will have had a blank verso so could
have become displaced on its own.
See longer notes.

Summary of the train of thought of the Sonnets in this text

(The titles here used to characterise each main sub-division of the thought are phrases taken from a sonnet in that group.)

SERIES ONE

Beauty's Rose

My fair friend's beauty is the perfect Rose, yet it is at the mercy of time. It is lent by nature, not his own to waste. To refute the charge that he is only in love with himself, he should beget children to preserve for us all the perfect form which he embodies (1 - 14). The verse my love bears to him is a less happy kind of posterity (15 - 16), for who would believe it unless some living model of him survived? (17). And yet all temporal beauty and its progeny can be spoiled by time, while the beauty of art survives unaltered and transcends time (18 - 19, 55).

But Truly Write

As the scent of the Rose is its essence, which so long as it is not cankered can be preserved by the distiller, so my love's truth can be preserved by verse when his external beauty fades (54). Like a woman in face, he is not fickle at heart like them, but differs from them in constancy as Sun from Moon; yet I could wish he were a woman. Let him share the act of love with them, provided he keeps love itself for me (20). Let truth inform my poems also: I admit that he is human rather than perfect (21). We have exchanged pledges of lifelong love, but I am older than he, and I fear to lose him (22). I am afraid to speak out to his face, so my books must tell my love for me (23). To find his true image, see him through my eyes; and yet they cannot see down into his heart (24). Public favour among the great is a thing quickly lost; I care only about private faithfulness (25). My love as yet is little to offer, so I will absent myself until I can clothe it in words more worthily (26).

A Journey in my Head

Night and day his image obsesses me, days are weary in my absence from him and nights sleepless (27-8). Or if I dream I see an image of him so bright that it reminds me of the greater brightness of the reality (43). My body made of the heavy elements is absent from him, though my eye has a painting of him to look at; my airy elements of mind and heart are with him in spite of distance (44-7). I can wait patiently for the time to return, knowing that my best jewel is safe at home (52). His real self is hidden behind many images; Adonis and Helen, male and female beauty are his shadows, but as the Idea behind them he must be unchangingly true at heart (53). When I return, the two horses of spiritual and physical love will run to meet him, but the first will far outrun the second (50-51).

Sweet Thief: A Plea Against My Self

The world makes an outcast of me, but you my friend console me for all (29). Many of my friends are dead, but I seem to regain them in you, and I now love you solely instead of those I have lost (30-31). When I in my turn die, I shall not mind you valuing other poets' work more highly for their art, if you value mine uniquely for my love (32).

But your love for me has clouded over in its morning (33). You misled me with your promise of lasting favour; though you now shed tears of regret, you have caused me loss and disgrace which you cannot cure (34). Since my love of the thief is what makes me hate the robbery, I feel I must extenuate what you have done, and state your case instead of my own in the court Plea which follows (35).

I concede, then, that there are good reasons connected with your reputation why you should disown me publicly and cut short our times together (36). I can fancy that it is enough for me to enjoy reputation, prosperity and young blood vicariously through you (37). You owe me no gratitude, new commissions or literary monopoly, even though the public have liked my praises of you (38). Your honour from my work will be the greater if both of us seem detached and disinterested, so I am willing to lose our name for unity in love, to accept your wish for separation and in writing about you to make two persons out of one (39). My loves are now plural, but since they are all yours, I cannot blame you (though it is blameworthy) if you enjoy my love in one sense and reject it in another (40). Your youth and your beauty make it natural that you should indulge yourself, and of the two of you it is the lady who leads you on, but I grieve that you should have broken both parties' faith with me (41). You can profess to have taken her from me for my own sake, since my interests are at one with yours. I value her less than I do you (42). You yourself are the jewel I really fear to be robbed of; yet self-theft is no crime, I cannot deny your right to come and go freely (48). If you ever decide to withdraw your love from me entirely, I can bring forward no lawful reason why you should not. So there is no case before the court for you to answer (49).

So True a Fool

I cannot write with novelty like others, for my subject is always and only you (76). You are like food to me, sometimes plentiful, sometimes grudgingly or proudly shared with others, sometimes withheld so that I starve (75). As appetite returns daily, so my love should persist through this sad interim of starvation and not be discouraged (56). I am like a slave who must wait upon your choice of times to see me, and have no right to question what you do meanwhile or with whom (57-58). Your image at night keeps me wakeful, but my love not yours is what creates it, and keeps me wondering where you are and imagining you with others (61). I look in my mirror and think myself all that is admirable, but that is only because I see your image there instead of mine (62). When my friend's face is as lined as mine, the lines of my verse will yet rejuvenate him for future ages (63). But alas, canker can prevent the distiller preserving a rose, and my friend lives among those who infect him and sap his life-blood (67). His beauty is a survival from a past golden age, but the world which commends it is less kind about his conduct; the company he keeps is to blame; great beauty invites both the canker of vice and slander (68-70). If he is a reborn Phoenix, I wish I could identify portraits of him in past writers; but whatever their style, I am sure their models were no better, or their record would have survived recognisably (59).

(This 3rd edition reverts to the Quarto order here; there is little difference in the train of thought).

Sad Mortality

But all is flux, and perfection a brief zenith from which decline begins immediately (60). I cannot help but fear that my love too will be destroyed by time, that its jewel can belong securely only to the tomb: unless by some miracle poetry can preserve love (64-65). I do not mind death for myself, the dishonesty of these times has wearied me, but by dying I should desert my love (66). Once I am dead, my friend, you would do best to forget me; I do not want you to suffer, also if you lament me the world will mock you; I have done nothing to bring you credit (71-72). I am at the autumn and sunset of my days, my fire is dying (73). But console yourself when I am dead with this volume, for it contains the best of me, which was my love of you (74). *Envoi:* As your glass and timepiece show you that you must age and die, this half-filled book will teach you how to draw metaphors and morals therefrom. Fill the rest of it with similar reflections that you write or come across, and you will gain wisdom and much increase the book's worth (77).

[Presumably the notebook came back again to the poet in due course. If it came back because its dedication was refused by the patron, that would explain why the final Envoi does not re-present it directly to him.]

Summary of the train of thought of the Sonnets in this text

SERIES TWO

Resumption and prologue

Whichever of us dies first, I will be buried obscurely and you in a handsome tomb - no, not that new family vault of yours, but this verse, which can outlast any literal tomb (81).

Victors of My Silence

But I can hardly write of you, knowing that a greater spirit does so (80). Indeed, many now imitate me by praising you, but I who owe you most can best bear witness (78-79). You were free of course to commission more skilled poets, and you have grumbled at my silence; but flattery can only detract from you who do not need it (82-84). What I mean inwardly is worth more than what I and others have managed to say (85). My chief rival helped by a ghost has silenced me; but their skill alone could not have done so, it was your showing favour to poetry which took over my theme of love for you (86).

Farewell; I am not good enough for you and have never securely possessed you (87). I can make it easy for you to think me unworthy, can put you in the right for having forsworn our love, by telling a story of sins on my own side (88). *[The story follows at Q113-Q154.]*

I love you so deeply that I will take guilt and exile upon me to please you (89). Say openly now that you hate me, then the other blows that are raining on me will seem nothing (90). You yourself and not the lesser things of life were all my joy, and are now my loss (91). But I am lucky that in a sense I cannot lose you, for I cannot remain alive without you, once I am certain that you have forsaken me (92).

How Like Eve's Apple

But what if you keep me living on by deceiving me, like a woman unfaithful to her husband? Your face may mislead me, for it is unable to show hatred (93). In that case you would be wise to deceive as well as possible, with both words and looks, for if I should go mad from suspicion I might speak ill of you (140). Do not drive me to that, which would put me in the wrong and so justify your treatment of me. Best then if you

160

say frankly that you love elsewhere, and kill me quickly with a look of hatred, instead of glancing aside like a flirting girl (139). Some can shed their glances all abroad like the Sun fertilising flowers, can move others but not be moved and so do no harm, impartially in command of their faces and feelings. But those who are themselves merely flowers contract the canker of vice that way (94). Even canker seems beautiful in you, scandals talked about your wantonness seem venial and charming just because it is yours. But you cannot expect to confuse people's judgments like this for ever (95). It is this disguise of wolf as lamb that gives you power to mislead so many. (Original final couplet probably missing (96).) (See *ad loc*).

[A year of absence has followed when I have played with other flowers as poor substitutes for you (97-99). The missing thread of thought from here to Q113, introducing his self-exile (promised in Q89) could have been something like 'I run from you in fear, no longer able to tell wolf from lamb, crow from dove.' Qs 97-9 revert to the metaphor of flowers (which was used in Qs 94-5); they may have been written as a brief summary of the Dark Lady episode after it was excised from here.]

I Mistake My View

Since I left you, my longing for you blinds me to reality; I impose your image on everything I see, ugly as well as beautiful, Crow as well as Dove. Thus my faithfulness is the real cause of my coming infidelity (113). Have my eyes the alchemist's power to turn an evil thing into your sweet self? No, they serve me a poisoned love-potion disguised as what I long for, and first gladly poison themselves (114). What has happened to my eyes that they see fairness where the world sees the opposite? Love's long tears have blinded them and they now dote on a mistaken object (148). My love is fever-sick and lusts for more of this poison, even if it means death as reason my doctor has warned. First comes madness, and what I say is raving, for the love I have been calling fair I now see is black as hell (147). Lust is hell and madness, a poisoned bait, craved and yet loathed as soon as swallowed (129).

This black mistress of mine is no Sun; she is far from an aesthetic ideal, though as good as any other over-praised woman (130). Many deny her beauty, but she knows that my present dotage counts her my best jewel; anyway it is just her conduct that makes her black (131). Her blackness puts the Sun out of countenance, and makes me think it the only colour to love (132). Since true Beauty who was fair has been dethroned by imitations, my mistress is black as if in mourning over such dishonesty, and it suits her so well that the world now begins to acclaim her the true goddess (127). When the world could not hold out, how could I? I forswore the love of woman which is the earthly Venus, but my mistress is heavenly, having just been deified. The fair Sun to whom I breathed my vow can remit it (and if he broke it first, cannot hold me to blame). (*Pilgr. 3*). Faith and forswearing, truth and lies are confused when I lie with my mistress (138). I have transferred my love from truth to error; heart and eyes pretend not to see that she is an unsightly whore (137). No, my eyes and other senses do perceive her faults, but it is too late for my heart to unlearn its slavery (141).

A Torment Thrice Threefold

I deserve punishment for my love, but she has not the right to rebuke it as she does, since she lusts for others as much as I for her (142). She gets what she wants, why should not I? All the parties are Will personified *[One of the meanings of Will was lust]* so surely it is all one who sleeps with her. Let me still have a share in her because of my name (135-136). She chases her Will like a henwife while I chase her (143). I love them both, the fair man and the dark woman who are my good and evil angels; but I dread that the one has enticed the other into her hell (144). I mind the injury to my friend, my other self, worse than my own; I admit now that he is lost to me; you have us both in prison, cruel woman (133-134). How can you say I do not love you, when I side against my other self in serving you? (149). You make me dispraise the Sun and see defect as merit (150). It is your fault if my body betrays my best self with you, for you exact the dues owed to another, and make me think that to serve you in bed is the same thing as to triumph in true love's tournament (151). You break faith both with him and me, but I am worse, for in swearing that you are my fair true love I mock all that I have written of love, fairness and constancy (152). There is a bath which claims to cure Cupid's brand and the consequent strange maladies; but my mistresses' eye undoes the cure (153-154). *The Quarto text fails to rhyme; 'eye' may mean female sex organ.*

Not Mine Own Fears

Give up dark and base subjects, my Muse, and return to your true theme. Rise to your feet (100), and defend yourself in court *[The closing scene seems set in a court of love like that before which Series One's Plea was argued.]* for this lapse. Let me show you the sort of thing you should say (101). I stopped singing about my friend because there were too many songsters, not because my love became any less (102). The bare theme, my friend in his own person, is better than all I can say of him (103). Our friendship has survived three winters, but it does not age for me (104). It is not idolatry that I always praise him; I leave out what differs from the ideal, because that is all my love is concerned with. I have found ways of saying all I mean about the relation of fair looks, truth and kindness (105). Past descriptions of perfect beauty were only a prophecy of my love (106), and the world-soul which longs for fulfilment of that prophecy can now take heart along with me. The imprisonment is over, the Moon's lethal power ended, the forecasts of my death falsified, and all is happy peace (107).

What else is there to be said, dear boy - I take it you understand all? I see now that perfect love did not die in the past, neither in the world's past nor our own, but it can be for ever renewed (108).

Love's Not Time's Fool

You exclaim that I was false to you? Sooner to my own soul, for you are my all. My journey away from you had a planned and timely ending (109). I admit I am only an actor; I have been acting a part in this absence from you; worse adventures in love were to prove you my best one (110). My lot in life is an unreserved, corrupting profession.

If I have been sick, you are the person to cure me (111). Scandals that are spread about me count for nothing if only you think kindly of me and judge me for yourself (112). Yes, I have told untruths - in boasting that my love for you had reached perfection. True love is always developing, it knows no finiteness (115). It is a marriage of the mind which no marriage-law can forbid; no desertion by the other can make it change heart; if there is any such thing, it defies time to the end (116).

Reply and summarise your charges. I have failed in my duty to write about you, have left you and consorted with others; worse can reasonably be guessed? Yes, but it was done as a trial of your love (117). I disciplined my taste for your love by sampling the opposite; all was for reasons of policy in love (118). The antidote to you which I tried sickened me in earnest; my dream of pleasure was hell-sent, a fever, a madness, an affliction of the eyesight; now my ruined love for you is rebuilt better than before (119). If you have suffered from my seeming desertion as I once did from yours, you have been through hell. Let the fault of each entitle the other to absolute discharge (120).

As for the world's case against me, why forgo what one does not feel to be wrong when they will accuse one just the same? I am true to myself, and their different sexual morals may be worse than mine (121). I am not impressed by fashions, which are only old things revived (123). If my love were all fashion and expediency, its begetter might justly disown it, and it would have wilted in adversity (124). I care nothing for the pageant of prestige occasions, whose platforms for vast themes are soon dismantled; I am free from ulterior motives, and this offering of myself is sincere (125).

You who now seem to be Nature's triumph over Time, flourishing the more as your lovers wane, never trust her, for she will make her peace with Time in the end by yielding you up (126).

Envoi: The notebook you gave me is full now, and I have made bold to give it away. Its words were but a poor record of a love which I shall never forget (122).

Supplement

Q128

How oft when thou my music music play'st,
Upon that blessed wood whose motion sounds
With thy sweet fingers when thou gently sway'st
The wiry concord that mine ear confounds,
Do I envý those jacks that nimble leap
To kiss the tender inward of thy hand,
Whilst my poor lips which should that harvest reap
At the wood's boldness by thee blushing stand.
To be so tickled they would change their state
And situation with those dancing chips,
O'er whom thy fingers walk with gentle gait,
Making dead wood more blest than living lips.
Since saucy jacks so happy are in this,
Give them thy fingers, me thy lips to kiss.

Q prints this in the Dark Lady context of Series II, but its Quarto mis-spelling of 'thy' as 'their' (lines 11 and 14) occurs only in Series I. It has no preoccupations of either gender, colour or morality in common with either Series, unless its affinity with Q8 could mean it was addressed to H.W.

Diagram of the Text

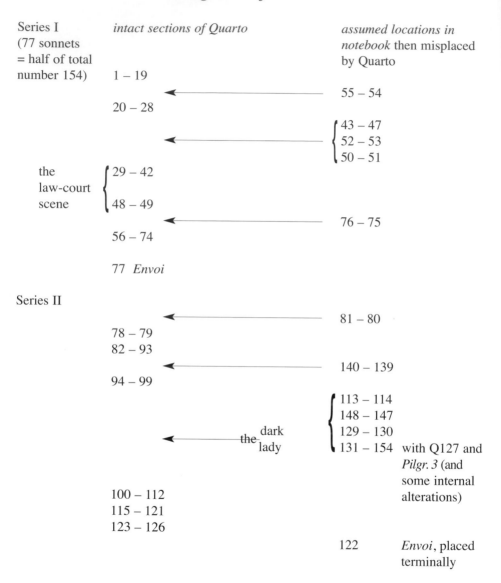

Series I
(77 sonnets
= half of total
number 154)

intact sections of Quarto

*assumed locations in
notebook* then misplaced
by Quarto

1 – 19

55 – 54

20 – 28

43 – 47
52 – 53
50 – 51

the
law-court
scene

{ 29 – 42

48 – 49

76 – 75

56 – 74

77 *Envoi*

Series II

81 – 80

78 – 79
82 – 93

140 – 139

94 – 99

113 – 114
148 – 147
129 – 130
131 – 154

the dark
lady

with Q127 and
Pilgr. 3 (and
some internal
alterations)

100 – 112
115 – 121
123 – 126

122   *Envoi*, placed
terminally

This diagram is over-simplified. What is in fact assumed is that a continuous section of ten leaves was cut out of the notebook's Series I (= mainly the stolen mistress law-court scene). Seven of these leaves (Qs. 29-42) were placed between Q27 and Q28 but set into print after Q28 because it was obviously twinned with Q27. Two leaves (Q48-9 and Q50-51) were placed between the intact pages bearing Q47 and Q52 (a bitter gesture since Q48 dynamites Q52's jewel chest). The tenth successive excised leaf Q76-75 was placed where it obscures Q74's link with the *Envoi* Q77. Then an eleventh leaf was cut from between Q19 and Q20 to bridge the gulf that had been described by the notebook between Q53 and Q56.

In this text there is no renumbering, Quarto numbers are used preceded by the letter Q. A manuscript notebook is postulated with pages that had one sonnet on each side, so that each retains at least one of its Quarto neighbours (with a very few exceptions). The majority retain both (it is the many traces of connected thought in the Quarto which justify re-ordering). Placing Q1 on a left-hand page brings nearly all the closely linked thought-pairs onto facing pages.

The division into two Series is evidenced not only by the Notebook Sonnets but by an edition often thought worthless, Benson's of 1640. He jumbles the sonnets extensively but only within their own Series. Had he acquired Thorpe's foul papers? A difference of handwriting between the two Series is likely because only Series I frequently misprints "thy" as "their" in the Quarto.

Reversed pages. This text assumes that leaves cut out of the notebook were reversed in seven instances. There is no need to take that as due to accident. I reversed them because that made the train of thought much clearer, and have assumed that the poet wished to conceal his sequence of thought which would be why he reversed them.

Recent topic	*New topic*
Uncritical praise	Without truth, beauty is perishable
Q55	Q54
The friend is a Sun	But sunsets must happen
Q76	Q75
We must both remember our mortality (cf. Q77)	Rival poets
Q81	Q80
Farewell to the friend	Begins to see the friend as female
Q140 (a threat to go mad, taken up by Q147)	Q139 taking up Q93
Transition to a delusory love	Delusion becomes complete
Q148	Q147
?A gentle context (possibly Q128 the harpsichord player)	Angry mood, making a close thought-pair with Q141
Q138	Q137
Still in earnest	Of nugatory content
Q146	Q145 (followed by the merely bawdy Qs 153-4)

LONGER NOTES ON SOME SONNETS

Dedication   This could not have been addressed unequivocally to H.W. since it is clear from the second notebook sonnet Q122 that there had been no question of re-submitting the text after its return to the poet half-way through. Anything Shakespeare authorised would be likely to have multiple meanings; a) H.W.'s initials are reversed to avoid association with *Avisa;* b) a composite personification of the friendship as Will-Henry could be meant; c) the widower of H.W.'s mother William Harvey could have been the source of the manuscript, see Longer Note on Q122. "Mr" does not suggest a peer, but one notes that Ben Jonson dedicating to a peer a few years later wrote "I dare not change your title".

    "Onlie begetter" must be Shakespeare's phrase; it attributes godhead (cf. Q110 "a God in love"), and only the Muse can say who parented her children (the same metaphor is used in twelve sonnets, Qs 16, 32, 38, 59, 72, 76, 77, 78, 82, 86, 103, 124). The phrase also carries the meaning that there is only one addressee, not two as would appear from Series II. The initials T.T. after the dedication are taken to mean the publisher Thomas Thorpe (if it were impermissible to initial other men's words the British Civil Service would be in trouble).

Q20   This notorious sonnet is the only one in Series I that can be found shockingly homosexual despite its partial disclaimer. (Series II delights to shock, but only in a hetero context). In fact it can come across as calculating and artificial, after which Q21 breathes the fresh air of sincerity. The sexist ideology here was the patron's not the poet's (see Introduction IV), and the sequence will very soon fault him for lacking the masculine constancy and straight dealing he is here praised for. Perhaps an elite set of young people is always liable to generalise about sex and gender, and their older friend may here be playing their game for his own deeper purposes. The last line's divorce of sex from love is abominated in Series II, as not "use" but "misuse", "abuse". The coining of a mistress from the friend in the coming law-court scene was not entirely Shakespeare's invention; John Clapham's *Narcissus* (printed in 1591) saw H.W. as in love with his own shadow-self. "Passion" in line 2 could then mean love poetry, it did not yet connote hysterical or "over the top" emotion.

Q23   Reads like an early sonnet, dense with meanings that outstrip his language (did he write "or some fierce bear" and get laughed at? Bear-baiting was adjacent to the Rose theatre). "Books" must mean the works dedicated to Southampton (Shakespeare did not dedicate any plays), and its alteration to "looks" by some who hold the Pembroke theory is editorially inexcusable as well as a failure to understand the poem. Poetry at that date in history was still for all but the highly educated essentially something spoken not written, and certainly so for an actor and the first literate member of his family. Written books are a mere dumb-show - but they can communicate in private which is a priceless merit, they can serve like a secret exchange of glances between lovers.

Line 1 "imperfect" includes not knowing his lines, cf. Bottom "Take pains, be perfect". A merely logical sonnet would have had a perfect actor for contrast in the sestet, instead of the paradox that a dumb-show can be more eloquent. See p.78.

Q53   On Adonis see Introduction I. The Helen image is sinister, since she stands for infidelity. But the stated topic is "strange shadows". The Greek poet Stesichorus was stricken blind when he said that Helen's beauty was belied by her conduct. He regained his sight when he said that it was only her 'eidolon', a phantom coined from her, that went to Troy. This surely inspired the Series II mistaking of a crow for a dove, a phantom that personified unfaithful lust for the real friend.

Qs48-49   This marvellous pair of sonnets, equally eloquent in tenderness and bitter irony, ends the 'plea against my self'. Jewels locked away are a marvellous correlative for absence, but Q48's sestet defies the metaphysical convention that one writes about the vehicle and not its tenor; the language appropriate to a chest only becomes fully poetic when humanised - "Thee have I not locked up in any chest Save where thou art not, though I feel thou art, Within the gentle closure of my breast". In Q49 there is superb ambivalence about "ensconce me here Within the knowledge of mine own desert" viz. how great it is, though he tells the court he has none. "No cause", because self-theft is not a crime, and because "the strength of laws" does not recognise such love as binding. Also he has promised to speak on his adversary's side, out of loyalty to him.

Q67   One of the most beautiful sonnets in its use of word sounds in the octave. The opening fricatives are protest sounds (as the BBC knows, cf. File on Four, Face the Facts); "indirectly seek" - the syllable 'ect" is an indirect approach to the rhyne-sound "eek".

Line 1 ff. e.g. Nashe in *The Choosing of Valentines* was persuading H.W. to visit brothels.

Line 6 ?easier sense would be "seeming".

SERIES II

Q80ff.   "silence" (Q83.9) presumably = failure to complete his commission which was to fill the whole notebook. Also implied is some criticism of the quality of Series I. The long poems to H.W. had been stylish and elegant; close personal relationship (which had to include reproaches) was much more refractory material, while evoking new aspects of his genius and of that of the sonnet form, which he shows need not be a highly tooled miniature – it is known that he wrote fast like a river in spare, "never blotting a line".

Q86   Collaboration between a living writer and a ghost strongly suggests Marlowe (who died in 1593), as does the opening line's admiration, and Chapman ("his" in line 4?) who boasted that he had access to Marlowe's ghost for completing the unfinished *Hero and Leander* (see Introduction III). line 10 "gulls" suggests the ghost is the superior poet (what thrilled Keats was probably Homer rather than his translator – though Chapman's worst vice was digression, which a translator is precluded from).

    Line 12 Any encouragement shown to Chapman would have been intolerable in view of the content of his second "Hymn" (Q85.7). Hence Farewell follows, and a promise to accept the role of scapegoat which Chapman had allotted him, by telling a story in which he is the culpable friend.

Q92   If I knew I had lost you I could die. But what if you dissemble, like a woman (Q93)? Courtly love-death and loss of livelihood could both be in mind. The end-stopped lines convey world-weariness. In line 14 "and yet" must be subordinate, "without my knowing it".

Q93ff.   The metaphor of "deceived husband" justifies moving Qs140-139 to here. Addressed to the Dark Lady the threat to go mad and speak ill of her becomes nonsense, for when it is fulfilled in Q147 it consists only in calling her black, which is specified as her natural colouring.

    Lines 1, 4 mean "I shall live wrongly trusting", *not* a guess that the wife may be true after all. Not "your looks are always with me", for she has a roving eye, but = you can look at me without showing your duplicity.

Q139   The transvestite view of the friend started (for this Series) by Q93 comes on gradually; I have put "her" and "she" (lines 10-11) into inverted commas, but "dear heart" is echoed by Q95 which is certainly to the friend, and it is a rare and tender address in Shakespeare.

Q96   The thread of thought breaks off here in the Quarto, and the couplet borrowed from Q35 looks like a summing up of the excised adventure (as do Qs97-99) – I shall put myself in the wrong again by saying that I am the friend who is at fault. If the Orsino couplet stood here in the notebook it must have been borrowed by the later play; its animal imagery links closely with Q113. A known overlap between plays and sonnets is Q94.14 quoted in the sonnet-writing scene of *Edward III* (did both quote a folk-lore saying?) and a possible one later here, see *Pilgr. 3* (p.112).

Q113-4, 148-7, 129-130 "I mistake my view" (Q148.11)

The component parts of this amazing bridge passage come from three different sites in the Quarto. The first pair must belong in Absence not in Return where Q places them. The third pair introduce the dark mistress as they do in Q. Placed between these outer pairs and reversed, the leaf Q148-7 leads compulsively into the Lust sonnet by its death-wish defiance of the doctor, while Q148 leads from projecting the friend's image onto good and bad alike (Q114) to eyes exhausted by tears mistaking the bad for the good. It is beyond belief that poems so closely integrated could have been written without interdependent relationship to each other.

My first edition was found shocking by some, I think by William Empson though he saw sense in the re-ordering, because of its bald admission that the friend is mistaken for a whore, or vice versa. But insult is not the name of the game, it is not a game, it is schizophrenia, a loss of bearings about what is real and what is not. The friend forfeits his identity by his breach of faith: "this is and is not Cressid". The reversibility is frightening: not to know whether Crow has dressed up as Dove or the Dove was a Crow in disguise. Logic is affronted, has no option but the opposite, in gender, colouring and erotic idealogy. Does the witch of lust oust Platonic love or was that only a disguise for the witch – which is Duessa and which is Una? Surely Shakespeare's empathy with human dilemmas was too wide not to include this one. The dark lady fails as a substitute essentially because she is not an individual person (unless perhaps in Q138) but a tool of witchcraft or an avatar of Vénus tout entière à sa proie attachée. The misogny is generic, the widespread view that the deity which torments both genders is female not male. But the wonderful couplet of Q148 adds the opposite theology – Psyche feared that Cupid came to her only in darkness because he was ugly. *Beauty and the Beast* has that theology, the Papageno incident in *The Magic Flute* the commoner one. Spenser's and Shakespeare's blaming of witchcraft rather than deity is found in these lines from Chapman's *Euthymia*,

> Like errant knights who by enchantments swerve
> From their true lady's being, and embrace
> An ugly witch with her fantastic face.

(Lines 456-8)

Modern psychology recgonises falling in love on the rebound, from a failed or over-idealised love to a faulty but at least accessible substitute. "As rare as any she" (Q130) means not rare at all. But before the therapy worked in Q119 there were depths to be plumbed. And of course the Quarto text denies that there was therapy.

171

Q149-152	A ding-dong of recriminations in which his wish to keep the love of his alter ego, who has vainly tried to bail him out, seems to be resented by the mistress as a failure in love to her. Does she now hate both of them for divided loyalties?
Q151	This sonnet is not to be dismissed as sex *et praeterea nihil,* the thought and images are complex. Cupid is too young to have carnal knowledge, yet only love can beget moral understanding. The lover rises and falls as in a tourney, at the name of love, but she is the wrong goddess, to win whom can only mean defeat and the body's enslavement.
Q152	Easiest to understand in terms of the *L.L.L.* "bed-vow" to abstain from sex; but may well allude to instances of cheating which the preceding sonnets have not made explicit. As a climax to serious moral charges and self-accusations, the couplet "I have lied by calling you better looking than you are" comes as embarrassing bathos. Unless it refers to the mistake of identity which began the whole episode, and means "I have mistaken you for someone else who was fair".
Q45	Seems meant to be slight by virtue of its 4-beat lines. line 14 did she perhaps hate his patron?
Q107	It is hard to see why this has been thought to relate to the death of a queen: moons survive eclipses, it is for sublunary beings that they augur death or disaster. The diva triformis of Asia Minor is older and more powerful than Venus, she is Artemis (moon) as virgin, sex goddess, mother, and Hecate the witch: "she comes more near the earth than she was wont And makes men mad" (*Othello* 5.ii.108). It is surely the mistress whether man, woman, witch or goddess who has been eclipsed, and Q147's danger of death is over.
Q117-119	The prosecution which began in Q109, resumes more forcefully. The defence is the need to show that "drugs poison him who so fell sick of you". Q119 recovers from all the Dark Lady perils - the love potion and blindness in Q148, the madding fever of Q147 which leads to death; perjury, imprisonment and delusion are also out-lived.
Q121	His own sexual code, cf. p.xxvii. Line 7 "spies" – perhaps Lord Burleigh's, he had been very angry that H.W. would not marry his granddaughter, and said he did not want to marry at all. cf. Q125.13 "suborn'd informer".
Q124	Line 2 the only begetter of my love poetry might justly disown it. Line 4 the poems are treated as weeds or flowers according to how changing public opinion values them. I suggest the end criticises Catharists who thought death-bed repentance atoned for a bad life. It is changing with time that shows them fools. "Crime" overweighs "goodness" by its position in the line. See p.177.

Q126   Semantics and euphony both require exchanging the line-end nouns of the first two lines. "Sickle hour" collapses into less than four syllables, and the moon is a sickle for days not just hours. "Sickle power" – Time's scythe, the power of the sickle moon to grow by waning, the moon goddess's weapon of execution only briefly delegated to her servants such as H.W. (*Avisa* wields a sickle in the illuminated letters of the text.) Moon rather than sun rules the friend in this cold poem (not a sonnet), and twelve lines instead of fourteen warns of midnight.

Q122   The second Notebook Sonnet, see p.xiii and passim. It can be moved on its own because it will have had a blank verso in the notebook; it was presumably sent to H.W. on its own. "Full character'd" implies the book which was half full in Q77 is now full. Quite apart from the contents of Series II, there could have been no re-dedication of the whole when the first half had been returned to sender. It sounds like reassurance against libel that hje says he keeps no copy (though a filled book is an "idle rank" – inferior category of thing – than memory, which he cannot be ordered to erase). Unlike Q126 this conveys warmth of feeling – "so long as brain and heart . . . subsist".

     Line 12 "to give them from me": possibly to the "private friends" who according to Meres had access to them. It has been guessed that the notebook could have been given to H.W.'s mother, and returned to the author when her widower third husband William Harvey died (see note on Dedication). The reference to her in the Sonnets (Q3.9-10) is affectionate; she could have asked for the sonnets that urge him to marry. She said of her son "he is never kind to me", and she excused her estrangement from his father by saying he treated his manservant Dymock "like a god" (so gay love may have been part of his legacy to his son. That makes it the more unjust that Chapman's Hymn portrayed Shakespeare as Vice leading a young man's Virtue astray).

The Interplay of Logic and Emotion in Shakespeare

(This is the text of a lecture intended for an Oxbridge undergraduate audience but never delivered. It was written after retirement from the Cambridge University English Faculty, and incorporates much material from lectures given for them at earlier dates.)

There is or rather was, a scholar called John Crowe Ransom, who found himself able to condescend to Shakespeare's intelligence. He wrote some good poems, but our concern is with his criticism. He praises one of the more old-fashioned, hyperbolic sonnets, no. 55, and then calls it "not quite intelligent enough to be metaphysical"! Ransom disliked what he called "the poetry of the feelings" because it "taints us with subjectivism", sentimentality and self-indulgence". I wonder how he thought any dramatist could hold an audience for five minutes if he could not convey how his characters feel, especially at climaxes. Ransom rates Spenser's sonnets better than Shakespeare's because he says they are "more logical". I shall take that up later on, along with the question of metaphysical style, because the Sonnets are my own field of special knowledge; but the points I want to make apply throughout Shakespeare's work, from the largest to the smallest scale, the five-act play to the single sentence.

Logic happens out of time, drama happens in time; logic is static, drama is dynamic. Coleridge has a marvellous comment on the Shakespearean sentence: he writes, "His intellectual action is wholly unlike that of Ben Jonson or Fletcher. They see the totality of a sentence or passage, and then project it entire. Shakespeare goes on creating and evolving B out of A and C out of B and so on, just as a serpent moves, which makes a fulcrum of its own body, and seems for ever twisting and untwisting in its own strength." That contrasts what is simultaneous with what changes and evolves. The simultaneous and timeless can be described in any order you like, whereas for a developing action the temporal order is of the essence of the matter: that Cordelia dies five minutes before Lear and not five minutes after. And the same applies to sentences, which when spoken aloud are always happenings in time. I once knew the Shakespearean actor Robert Harris, who was a big name before his power to remember his lines deserted him, he told me that often when he read a Shakespeare speech to himself he didn't understand it, but the moment he spoke it aloud he understood. When I translated Sophocles' *Philoctetes* for my Cambridge undergraduates to act, one sentence came out terribly flat, as "Aren't you afraid of the Greek army?" We had to turn it round and copy the Greek order: "Greece has an army – aren't you afraid of it?" Logically that makes no difference, but only the second word order gets the fact that the sentence is a threat, a crescendo towards the idea of fear. So temporal order will often be crucial in the examples I give.

Most of us have enough trouble getting logic and psycho-logic to pull in the same direction in what we write. What fascinates me in Shakespeare, and it is surely something which could only be done by a mind which had complete command of both modes of thought, is that he can somehow contrive a double whammy by letting the two things pull in opposite directions. To give first a very simple example, in the last scene of the play Hamlet says "it is such a kind of gain-giving as would perhaps trouble a woman". ("Gain-giving" means misgiving). The logical gist of that is "I am not a woman, so no problem". The psychological undercurrent is just the opposite: "I have got to fight a duel and heaven help me, I am feeling like a woman". One of the most horrific things said anywhere in the plays is said by a character who thinks he is being reassuring. The logic of what he says is reassuring. In the last scene of Richard II, Exton comes in to the newly crowned Bolingbroke with two assistants carrying something heavy, and he says "Great King, within this coffin I present Thy buried fear". It's like the entrance of Banquo's ghost: a frisson of horror. That ghost haunts three further plays, until Henry V prays:

> Not today, O Lord,
> O not today, think not upon the fault
> My father made in compassing the crown!
>   . . . I have built
> Two chantries, where the sad and solemn priests
> Sing still for Richard's soul.

(Daringly sigmatic, that). Why weren't Shakespeare and his cast arraigned for high treason for acting Richard II on the eve of the Essex rebellion? The powers that be must have realised that its overall effect on the London public would be deterrent, bringing home the enormity of regicide. Exton could so easily have sounded genuinely reassuring: thy fear, great king, is buried, with more spadefuls of words dumped on top of that; a coffin ought not to be above ground. At the same time, a buried fear is more threatening than an acknowledged one; Shakespeare knew his Freud! The word order is (as so often) the secret here, because drama happens in time, King Lear fighting *hysterica passio* says "Down, thou climbing sorrow". He orders it down and it climbs, like seasickness. It disobeys him; he has abdicated, and nothing obeys him. The other way round, "Thou climbing sorrow, down!" – that would have been a success story. Shakespeare always knew which end of his Coleridgean snake-sentences had the fangs in it.

There's a subtle passage in *Coriolanus* which isn't a matter of word order, but of its being essential to work out the logic of what is said before one sees what Shakespeare is up to psychologically; and it could only have been written by a mind that had complete command of both modes of thought. Volumnia, the mother of Coriolanus (who is here called Marcus as he hasn't yet earned his title) is what my grandparents' generation called a "strong-minded woman", and I'm sure John Crowe Ransom would have approved of the effect of her no-nonsense masculine toughness on the woolly-minded Shakespeare; she actually makes him come out with a sum which adds up correctly. She is talking to her son's wife Virgilia, and she says: "Hear me profess sincerely: had I a dozen sons, each in my love alike, and none less dear than thine and my good Marcus, I had rather had eleven die nobly for their country than one voluptuously surfeit out of action". Splendid, eleven plus one equals a dozen. But – she's got the figure of speech wrong, hasn't she? If I said to you, I so much disapprove of gambling that if I had £10 to spare I would rather give £9 to Oxfam than spend £1 on the national lottery, you would say "Hi, you've cheated; you still have the £1 in your pocket which you could surreptitiously spend on the lottery". The correct paradigm for that figure of speech is all or nothing, "I would rather give the whole £10 to Oxfam", then you have made the alternative which you deprecate impossible. So what is Volumnia really doing? She is magnanimously offering up to the god of battle her eleven imaginary sons, and mentally reserving her one real son, because she cannot do without him. They have a deeply symbiotic relationship – she doesn't mind his being wounded, she is quite sadistic about that, but she cannot do without him, and in fact when he is exiled she goes mad. So the possessive mother is betrayed by her disingenuous arithmetic to those who have ears to hear, while she thinks that that is what proves her unpossessive. The author does not delay self-advertisingly to point this out: *ars est celare artem*. I diagnosed this passage for myself but if anyone has met the point in print do please let me know.

I suppose Coriolanus is nobody's favourite play, but it has a highly intellectual theme, which does not square with Crowe Ransom's thesis of an unintellectual writer. It's about self-cancellation, both of the play and of its hero, because the title which defines both is withdrawn when having won it by conquering Corioli the man proceeds to fight *with* those he conquered against Rome. "The man was noble, But with his last attempt he wiped it out", Volumnia imagines people saying. The play's politics also balance on a knife-edge; I don't myself think they are self-cancelling, but when it was acted in Paris and Moscow in the 1930s the Fascists said it was a Communist play and the Communists said it was a Fascist play. I wonder if it, among other things, meant to say that courage is self-cancelling unless it serves a consistent and worth-while purpose beyond itself – as in that lovely remark of C.S. Lewis: "courage is the form of every virtue at its testing point". There's a sentence in the play which could have been a straightforward blank verse line: "It is held that valour is the chiefest virtue". But it isn't laid out like that, it's spread across a line-end: "It is held", end of line, "that valour is the chiefest virtue". That throws emphasis on "held" and invites one to question it, none the less because the line is run on and not end-stopped. You only get the force of a run-on line if you notice where the rhythmic break *should* have happened and didn't. My family used to love rushing through Bletchley station in an express train on pre-war journeys, and you only got a kick out of that if you actually saw the long platforms rushing by and being ignored.

Of course I'm not saying that the end of a line of verse is the most important place in it – that leads to the appallingly bad versing which listens to the rhyme-sounds and not to the mid-line sounds. The best lines are boat-shaped, another C.S. Lewis saying though I don't know if he originated it; the centre of gravity is in the middle. But prosody creates sub-units of time, just as a sentence or scene or sonnet does, and a terminal position in any unit must have something conclusive about it, to state a tautology. Admittedly the final couplets of the Sonnets are often curiously neutral in tone and content, as though he feels it too late to say anything new until he can start the next sonnet; my favourite remark by the prestigious editor Stephen Booth is that the sonnets' couplets are like Fortinbras in *Hamlet*, brought in at the end to tidy things up. But if they affect or clarify the tenor of the whole one should take notice. The rather obscure sonnet 124 ends by talking about "the fools of time Which die for goodness, who have lived for crime". The taste left in the ears is the word "crime"; they are fools to think a death-bed repentance can offset a life of wrong-doing. An anti-Catharist sentiment: Catharists believed in the practice of postponing repentance to the death-bed (there's more than a hint of Catharism about the young man in "A Lover's Complaint" who was arguably the same person as the Sonnet's friend). Logically the order is indifferent, it could have been "who lived for crime and yet for goodness die". That would have been exculpatory in tone, whereas I think the whole sonnet cryptically implies a rebuke to the friend for inconstancy while vindicating the poet against a charge of it. "If my dear love were but the child of state It might for fortune's bastard be unfather'd." "State" meaning policy, expediency: in that case you the begetter of my love poems could justly disown them. (That is one of a dozen passages which bear out that "only begetter" must have been Shakespeare's phrase not the publisher's; it would have stood on the title-page of the ms. notebook). "You who disown my love poems are the one of us who is fortune's time-server, not I." I gloss the meaning as love poems because of the plurals in line 4, "Weeds among weeds, or flowers with flowers gather'd"; they are treated as weeds or flowers according to the context or social or cultural or fashionable climate. For some gardeners (like me) wild poppies in the path count as weeds, in the beds they count as flowers. That could have been a country adage.

This is a digression – country sayings last an extraordinarily long time. When Ezra Pound's son came to Stratford on a pilgrimage of bardolatry and went walking with a local yokel, they passed a field of dandelions and the local man said "We call those golden boys chimney sweepers when they go to seed" – because a dandelion clock is like a sweep's brush. "Golden lads and girls all must As chimney sweepers come to dust." One spotlight of illumination like that is worth all the centrifugal analogies and associations of over-stocked critical minds.

To turn to individual sonnets, complete poems not just couplets – I mentioned that John Crowe Ransom thought Spenser's sonnets better than Shakespeare's because they are more logical. My own favourite among Spenser's which is *Amoretti* No. 18, I like for the irrelevant reason that it conveys vividly what it is like to argue with a structuralist. He is complaining of his lady-love, and he says:

> But when I plead, she bids me play my part.
> And when I weep, she says tears are but water:
> And when I sigh, she says I know the art,
> And when I wail she turns herself to laughter.

Not drowning but waving. Poor Stevie.

Now that structuralist terminology has given way to that of deconstruction, may I offer you my simile for Derida – that he is like those people who buy balloons in order to bust them. Then they hand you a limp piece of discoloured rubber and say "that is all there was to your balloon". A lie: my balloon had shape, colour and grace of movement, all of which have been destroyed.

Shakespeare's sonnet 23 is an outstanding example of purposive departure from the logical framework which it appears to promise. "As an unperfect actor on the stage, Who with his fear is put besides his part . . . So I for fear of trust" – the poet trying to declare his love is like an inexperienced actor who gags from nervousness. The sestet begins "O let my books be then the eloquence" – a lucidly logical framework of contrast between "I" and "my books" which can substitute for my stumbling embarrassment and speak like a perfect actor instead of an imperfect one. But what happens in the very next line? "O let my books be then the eloquence And dumb presagers of my speaking breast" – instead of a star performer we get a dumbshow, which one would expect to be even more inadequate than the victim of stage-fright to convey what is really meant. The snake of the metaphor has turned at a right-angle, something quite different from what logic expects and what the Metaphysicals do. Greater eloquence is now claimed for the stumbler, the lover speaking in his own person, than for the kind of eloquence that is accessible to the public whether in books or an expert performance.

Poetry was at that date still essentially something spoken and listened to aloud (and would Shakespeare's plays have lived so long if they hadn't been spoken aloud in every performance?). And yet he does want to recommend his love poetry, although it's only dumbshow on a silent page, so the final couplet has a marvellous further twist: (it's no mere Fortinbras, this one). "O learn to read what silent love hath writ, To hear with eyes belongs to love's fine wit." Written lines can serve like a silent secret glance exchanged by two lovers who don't want to give themselves away in a roomful of strangers. There couldn't possibly have been that density of meaning in a poem which had merely followed through the logical scaffolding. Sonnet 23 is not without faults, it is probably a very early one and has weak lines, but it shows unprecedented ambition as to what can be expressed by the sonnet form, partly through metaphors which evolve and are self-revising.

Those scholars who call the sonnets "literary exercises" seem not to have noticed the object of the exercise, the expressiveness they gain by departing from literary expectations. There is a lot of anti-Petrarchanism in them, rejection of the extravert and hyperbolic which magnifies the lover or the beloved by magnifying external symbols, which are so much easier to write about than private, personal material. Take the two sonnets about slavery, 57 and 58. A traditional treatment would go to town on the theme of slavery: I let you put your foot on my neck, inflict dire punishments, if you ordered my death I would die to serve you, that sort of thing. What do these two sonnets actually complain of? Of having to "watch the clock for you"; for a whole hour – a "world without end hour" – you said you'd come back at four and you didn't come back till five – that is centuries ahead of its time in its realism, it's like a description of the painful threshold to a divorce. I can't ask you where you have been, when you'll come back, who you've been with. "But like a sad slave, sit and think of nought Save where you are, how happy you make those." The one unimportant word there is the word "slave"! at most it is a slang exaggeration, like saying "I'm dying to see you". "You yourself may privilege your time To what you will" – an otiose permission, surely, from a slave to a monarch. These two sonnets in fact convey powerfully how much intimacy there was before the friendship clouded over; it's unlikely that they convey that by mistake, and if they convey it by intention they are not literary exercises.

Another sonnet which is anti-Petrarchan and anti-Metaphysical is the jewel chest one, no. 48. The metaphor would traditionally evoke hyperbole, a lush description of jewels. This is one of the Absence sonnets, and for a start the jewels are shut away in a box, which is both paradoxical and a lovely objective correlative for absence. Then the sestet breaks that mould too, it disowns the metaphor or turns it through a right angle, which is the opposite of what the metaphysicals do. They of course tip the wink that their metaphor is not their ulterior subject, but they faithfully follow it through. Shakespeare's practice reminds me rather of a phrase from Vita Sackville West's *The Land*, "to throw away Each broken, each successive crutch". This sestet runs:

> Thee have I not locked up in any chest
> Save where thou art not, though I feel thou art,
> Within the gentle closure of my breast,
> From whence at pleasure thou may'st come and part.

(A zeugma makes 'from' cover 'to' in that fourth line.)

The human imagery ousts the metaphor even where it uses language common to both. These lines are not a literary exercise, and they are not "less intelligent" than metaphysical writing.

The earlier Sonnets are legalistic, argumentatitve, to suit his law-trained patron. In general his use of metaphor is cavalier about metaphor while the Metaphysicals are punctilious, and in this he is more like the Greeks. Homeric metaphor is a single lantern slide, it may be a rich and complex picture but once it is flicked away it has gone for good. This leads to tolerance of what slower imaginations would take as mixed metaphor; the successive images are "this or this" not "this and this". Thus Housman's brilliant parody of Aeschylus begins "Oh suitably attired in leather boots Head of a traveller". (Actually "head of so-and-so" was an accepted Greek verse periphrasis for "So-and-so", and who need worry about dressing So-and-so in boots). Later on the parody has a "slaughterhouse garnished with shipwrecks of cows", Shakespeare's one-off i.e. lantern-slide use of a 'far-fet' metaphor, especially when he crosses with seven-league boots from the very abstract to the very concrete, can have a shock impact like that of surrealism: Troilus – "Instance, oh instance! strong as Pluto's gates!" He rattles at the iron bars of what is irrefutable yet also a contradiction. The power of the image is subliminal, instantaneous, it would be ruined if prolonged. Leavis is at his silliest when he criticises Housman's *Reveille* in *Scrutiny 13* without seeing that it uses

Homeric not metaphysical metaphor. The burning ship of sunrise lasts only one verse and then is abolished by the slide of the trampled tent. The most beautiful metaphor I know in literature is at the end of Odyssey Book V, where the nearly drowned Odysseus curls himself in to a heap of dead leaves between two olive trees, and is likened to a smouldering ember which the farmer heaps round with ashes in his lonely upland farmstead so that it may last through the night. Leavis would have to exclaim "Oh dear, what happens to poor Odysseus when the housewife pokes up the fire next morning?" For he remarks sarcastically that "we mustn't ask" what happens to Housman's burning ship of sunrise later in the day. Metaphysical metaphor is an impressive culmination in one direction of a many-branched literary form, it should never be regarded as a one-way street.

Ben Jonson, whose logicality we saw Coleridge (unlike Crowe Ransom) damns with faint praise, faulted many lines of Shakespeare's by his own criteria, for example "Caesar doth never wrong but with just cause". "Do wrong" virtually means "cause harm" here, but the full answer is Portia's: Shylock's suit is just but wrong, morally repugnant. Shakespeare has so strong a sense of personal individuality that all his scenes are stereoscopic, whereas logic is monoptic. Things said not only characterise the speaker but demand to be registered by the ears of all the hearers, both on stage and in the audience. It is for the audience to realise the difference between two characters from the difference between the Duke's greetings to them in *M.M.* "My very worthy cousin, fairly met", – "Our old and faithful friend, we are glad to see you!" It is through the ears of silent Juliet that we should hear the Nurse say "I think it best you married with the County", and (while unsurprised though disappointed in the Nurse) we are shattered with Juliet by her loss of her one ally and realisation that from now on she stands alone. Pandarus saying of Troilus "He cannot bear it!" has for the hearer the authority of a consultant giving a fatal prognosis, whereas said in the first person it would just be a patient's self-pity. Compare and contrast a weak moment in Euripides' *Medea* where she says "Now my passions are conquering my reason" and sounds like a robot displaying its works.

All Shakespeare's characters inform on each other as well as on themselves, and so does the action of his plots. The last scene of *Twelfth Night* must be the most astonishing piece of stereoscopic stage-craft in the canon of world drama. The brother and sister appear on stage together and for the first time are revealed to be two people not one. At least four sub-plots are instantaneously dissolved from angst into happiness: Orsino realises his page has not double-crossed him but has served his love-suit to another instead of her own to him. Olivia realises she has not been jilted; Antonio realises his bosom friend has not after all cynically disowned him; Sir Andrew sees it is no wonder he lost the duel. Yet the joy of brother and sister at realising that the other has not been drowned takes centre stage and even dwarfs the sub-plots with its Prodigal Son quality "was dead and is alive again, Was lost and is found". Only the Malvolio sub-plot fails to dissolve into joy because the deception of him was malicious not accidental. Perhaps that is why Feste's final song is one of the saddest endings in Shakespeare's plays.

Postscript

Portraits of W.S.

The Droeshout on page vi though posthumous is the best authenticated because Ben Jonson who knew Shakespeare well said it was a good likeness. Several newspapers this spring have been featuring tarted up portraits which probably derive from what is called the Somerville miniature by Hilliard. The Somervilles were Stratford people who claimed to have commissioned a painting of W.S. after his retirement from the stage, but they could have acquired a copy of the Hilliard at an earlier date. The Parnassus plays of 1598-1600 tell that a portrait of W.S. was then current. The Somerville miniature was the basis of the frontispiece shown below which was used for the 1821 edition of Shakespeare's works. It shows a central plume of hair indicating a younger man than the Droeshout - if he balded early, perhaps much younger. It has been questioned whether W.S. was the sitter because the jaw does not show the striking width of the Doreshout, but that could be due to clever styling of the beard. Greene and Nashe in the early 1590s mocked W.S. for "starching his beard" so as to look more fashionably Italianate and less like a hefty countryman? The candid searching eyes are the same as in the Droeshout.

INDEX OF QUARTO NUMBERS

185

INDEX OF FIRST LINES

I grant thou were not married to my Muse,	83
I never saw that you did painting need,	84
If my dear love were but the child of state,	152
If the dull substance of my flesh were thought,	33
If there be nothing new, but that which is	62
If thou survive my well-contented day	44
If thy sould check thee that I come so near,	118
In faith, I do not love thee with mine eyes,	115
In loving thee thou know'st I am forsworn,	126
In the old black age was not counted fair,	111
Is it for fear to wet a window's eye	10
Is it thy will thy image should keep open	64
Let me confess that we two must be twain,	48
Let me not to the marriage of true minds	145
Let not my love be call'd idolatry,	136
Let those who are in favour with their stars	28
Like as the waves make towards the pebbled shore,	63
Like as, to make our appetites more keen,	147
Lo, as a careful housewife runs to catch	119
Lo in the orient when the gracious light	8
Look in thy glass, and tell the face thou viewest	4
Lord of my love, to whom in vassalage	29
Love is my sin, and thy dear virtue hate,	116
Love is to young to know what conscience is;	125
Mine eye and heart are at a mortal war,	35
Mine eye hath play'd the painter and hath stell'd	27
Music to hear, why hear'st thou music sadly?	9
My glass shall not persuade me I am old,	25
My love is as a fever, longing still	106
My love is strengthened, though more weak in seeming;	133
My mistress' eyes are nothing like the sun;	108
My tongue-tied Muse in manners holds her still,	86
No longer mourn for me when I am dead	74
No more be griev'd at that which thou hast done:	47
No, Time, thou shalt not boast that I do change:	151
Not from the stars do I my judgement pluck;	15
Not marble, nor the gilded monuments	121
Not mine own fears, nor the prophetic soul	138
O call me not to justify the wrong	96
O, for my sake do you with Fortune chide,	142
O, from what power has thou this powerful might	124

O, how I faint when I of you do write,   80
O, how much more doth beauty beautous sem   22
O, how thy worth with manners may I sing,   51
Or I shall live your epitaph to make,   79
O, lest the world should task you to recite   75
O, me, what eyes hath Love put in my head,   105
O, never say that I was false of heart,   140
O, that you were your self! but, love, you are   14
O thou, my lovely boy, who in thy hour   154
O truant Muse, what shall be thy amends   132
Or whether doth my mind, being crown'd with you,   104

Poor sould, the centre of my sinful earth   127

Say that thou didst forsake me for some fault,   90
Shall I compare thee to a summer's day?   19
Sin of self-love possesseth all mine eye   65
Since brass, nor stone, nor earth, nor boundless sea,   68
Since I left you mine eye is in my mind,   103
So am I as the rich, whose blessed key   37
So are you to my thoughts as food to life,   58
So is it not with me as with that Muse   24
So, now I have confess'd that he is thine   122
So oft have I invoked thee for my Muse,   81
So shall I live supposing thou art true,   94
Some glory in their birth, some in their skill,   92
Some say, thy fault is youth, some wantonness;   99
Sweet love, renew thy force; be it not said   59

Take all my loves, my love, yea, take them all;   52
That god forbid that made me first your slave,   61
That thou art blam'd shall not be thy defect,   73
That thou hast her, it is not all my grief,   54
That time of year thou mayst in me behold   76
That you were once unkind befriends me now,   149
The expense of spirit in a waste of shame   107
The forward violet thus did I chide: 102
The little Love-God lying once asleep   130
The other two, slight air and purging fire,   34
Then hate me when thou wilt; if ever, now;   91
Then let not winter's ragged hand deface   7
They that have power to hurt and will do none,   97
Thine eyes I love, and they, as pitying me,   110

189